A Glimpse of God

Debra Niswander

WestBow Press
A DIVISION OF THOMAS NELSON
& ZONDERVAN

Copyright © 2014 Debra Niswander.

All rights reserved. No part of this book may be used or reproduced by any means, graphic, electronic, or mechanical, including photocopying, recording, taping or by any information storage retrieval system without the written permission of the publisher except in the case of brief quotations embodied in critical articles and reviews.

WestBow Press books may be ordered through booksellers or by contacting:

WestBow Press
A Division of Thomas Nelson & Zondervan
1663 Liberty Drive
Bloomington, IN 47403
www.westbowpress.com
1 (866) 928-1240

Because of the dynamic nature of the Internet, any web addresses or links contained in this book may have changed since publication and may no longer be valid. The views expressed in this work are solely those of the author and do not necessarily reflect the views of the publisher, and the publisher hereby disclaims any responsibility for them.

Any people depicted in stock imagery provided by Thinkstock are models,
and such images are being used for illustrative purposes only.
Certain stock imagery © Thinkstock.

ISBN: 978-1-4908-2729-2 (sc)
ISBN: 978-1-4908-2730-8 (hc)
ISBN: 978-1-4908-2728-5 (e)

Library of Congress Control Number: 2014903565

Printed in the United States of America.

WestBow Press rev. date: 3/25/2014

The King James version, called the "Authorized Version" in England, was a revision of the Bishops' Bible on the basis of Beza 1598, with much direct borrowing from the English texts of Tyndale 1535 and of the Genevan Bible.

Scripture quotations, in this publication are from the HOLY BIBLE, NEW INTERNATIONAL VERSION® NIV® Copyright © 1973, 1978, 1984, 2011 by Biblica, Inc.®. Used by permission. All rights reserved worldwide.

Scripture quotations taken from the Amplified ® Bible, Copyright © 1954, 1958, 1962, 1964, 1965, 1987 by the Lockman Foundation. Used by permission.

Scripture quotations taken from the New American Standard Bible®, Copyright © 1960, 1962, 1963, 1968, 1971, 1972, 1973, 1975, 1977, 1995 by the Lockman Foundation. Used by permission.

Scripture taken from the New King James Version®. Copyright © 1982 by Thomas Nelson, Inc. Used by permission. All rights reserved.

Scripture taken from the New Century Version®. Copyright © 2005 by Thomas Nelson, Inc. Used by permission. All rights reserved.

Scripture quotations from THE MESSAGE. Copyright © by Eugene H. Peterson 1993, 1994, 1995, 1996, 2000, 2001, 2002. Used by permission of NavPress Publishing Group.

Scripture quotations marked (NLT) are taken from the Holy Bible, New Living Translation, copyright © 1996, 2004, 2007 by Tyndale House Foundation. Used by permission of Tyndale House Publishers, Inc., Carol Stream, Illinois 60188. All rights reserved.

Donehey, Mike & Ingram, Jason. "You are More". The Light Meets the Dark. CD. Lyrics © Sony/ATV Music Publishing LLC, Peer Music Publishing. 2010.

Cowart, Benji & Weaver, Michael David. "Redeemed". Love Come To Life. Lyrics © Warner/Chappel Music, Inc. 2012.

Contents

Preface xi
Acknowledgments xv

Part 1 – God, the Father.. 1
    He Is Our Father... 3
    He Is Ultimate Love.. 5
    He Forgives.. 7
    He Is Our Boss... 9
    He Is the Healer of Our Soul 11
    He Is the Alpha and the Omega—the Beginning
        and the End 13
    He Is Our Refuge and Strength 15
    He Is the Peacemaker 17
    He Is THE Answer 19
    I AM.. 21

Part 2 – God, the Son... 25
    Jesus: A Love Story 27
    Jesus: The Son's Love for His Father;
        the Son's Love for Us 29
    Jesus: The Giver of Second Chances, and Third
        Chances, and Fourth Chances, and 31
    Jesus: Our Freedom Fighter 33
    Jesus: His Scars, Our Healing...................................... 35
    Jesus: Was, Is, and Always Will Be 37
    Do You Know the Word of God
        (the Bible) and the Word (Jesus)?......................... 39
    Jesus: The Master Painter 41
    Jesus: Our Savior... 44
    Jesus: You Know Him as Savior; Do You Know
        Him as Lord? 47

Part 3 – God, the Holy Spirit 51
    Truth's Voice 53
    Signed, Sealed, and Delivered 55
    You've Got a Friend in Him 57
    Teacher 59
    Equipment Man 62
    Road Maps and GPS 65
    Don't Turn Off the Faucet 68
    You're Not Alone
        (Our Swimming Instructor—Our Strength) 71
    Our Conqueror 74
    Our Producer 77

Part 4 – The Fruit of the Spirit 81
    LOVE –
    A Perfect Love 85
    Choices 87
    A Shared Love 89
    A Broken Heart Healed 91
    JOY –
    Stuffed 95
    Eternal Optimist 98
    Behind the Clouds 101
    Who's Your Trustee? 104
    Living Trust 106
    PEACE –
    He Holds On to You Even When You Can't or
        Won't Hold On to Him 109
    The Conquering "C" 112
    The Conquering "C" (continued) 115
    Peace in Our Worries, in Our Fears,
        in the Unknown, in Our Hurts,
        in Our Prayers That Seem to Be No 117

PATIENCE –
Commitment: Gotta Run to Run 121
Endurance: I Want To! 124
Contentment: To Have or Have Not 127
Perspective: Who or What Are You Waiting On? 129
KINDNESS –
Honey 133
Nothing Random about It 136
What If 138
The Least of These 140
GOODNESS –
Permanent and Inseparable 143
Out of the Gutter 145
New Heart, New Eyes 147
The Goodness of God 150
FAITH –
I Know That I Know That I Know 153
Why I Write 156
A Little Boy, a Little Prayer, a Lot of Sun 158
A Sister's Faith 161
GENTLENESS/ MEEKNESS (HUMILITY) –
Meekness Is Not Weakness 165
Remember Where You Were 168
Some Humble Pie 170
In Awe 172
SELF-CONTROL –
God-Control 175
Stumbling 178
C.A.R.P. 181
To Die, Yet Live 184

A Final Thought 187

Preface

Dear Friends,

I was struck one day when I was rereading the story of Moses' encounter with God through the burning bush. I couldn't get over God's answer to Moses' question: Who should I say sent me? (I imagine Moses thought, *I can't tell them a burning bush sent me; they'll think I've gone nuts.*) Who do I tell them You are? How do I describe You? The fact that God answered Moses and the answer He gave inspired several of my devotionals. Even writing this, I just keep shaking my head. Moses was speaking directly to the Creator. The Being who caused *all* to come into existence had talked to Moses. What's more, God wanted Moses to know who He was. He wants all of us to know who He is. I truly wonder what was running through Moses' mind at that moment.

That got me thinking about the question Jesus posed to His disciples: Who do people say I am? The disciples had various responses as to how He was being described, but most of those were that Jesus was only a person. Then Peter answered, "Thou art the Christ, the Son of the living God" (Matthew 16:16 KJV). What a revelation! Did Peter really understand what he had just said? He was talking to God (face-to-face), telling God that God was God! I wonder what Peter must have been thinking.

What words do you use when you speak of God? How do you describe Him? This is the God who created everything, created man; who healed us through the stripes that crisscrossed His own body; who stopped at nothing, even His own death, to save us. I started these devotionals years ago in hopes of helping my boys learn more about who God is. It is I who has been learning the most.

Some of my devotionals were written during specific events in my life. Others developed over extended periods of time and were forged in the ordinary, everyday occurrences of living: a bad day at work, feelings hurt by a friend or family, a job found or lost, good and bad choices, lost keys, bad hair days, missed appointments, celebrations, and arguments with my kids, etc. Ordinary, everyday life we all go through at one time or another—all of which provided opportunities for me to experience the character of God and to find out who He is and how He wanted to help me through all those experiences.

This book only shows glimpses of the journey I am on. But it has been a revelation that everything in my life thus far, whether it seems good or bad, whether of my own doing or another's, is a lesson in learning who God is and making the choice to trust who He says He is and what He wants for my life. Some days it is effortless to trust in my Creator, and then there are days, as you can read on these pages, it was and is a struggle. The days I struggle I must go back to that choice—to believe who He says He is, to trust the plans He has for my life, whether I fully understand them or know all of them yet—and to rest in that.

The more I learn of Him, the more I want to know, and the more I also realize it will still only be a glimpse until I pass into eternity. But oh, what a glimpse! The more I write, the more I see my words pale in comparison to a true description of God and who He is and what He has done for me, for you, for all of mankind. My words fall short in adequately portraying how much He loves each of us. I come to grips each time I have written a devotional (and as I reread them still) of how unworthy I am. But at the same time, I am immersed with the knowledge that because of Christ's love and sacrifice, He redeemed me and now I am worthy to be called a child of the *most high and living God*. Often I have had to confess and repent while writing these devotions, but as you can see, each page reflects who I have found God to be: a Father, a friend, a lover, a Savior, and I could go on and on. And through these revelations, I have found and continue to find grace, mercy, and peace, and more.

That is what I want you, my friend, to see. I pray that you would see God on the pages of this book. I pray that even if you only see a glimpse, it will create a spark that would burn in your soul. I pray that in this spark, you would find *His* unconditional love, *His* unwavering peace, and *His* eternal hope. I want you to meet God, know God, talk to God, and have God talk to you. He longs to talk to you, to be your friend, to be your Savior. And if anything He has helped me to write here leads you to find that out for yourself, then I am truly blessed.

As I told a friend of mine once (and it holds true for each of you as well), it is more important to me that you have a relationship with Jesus than you have a relationship with me. For if you forget me, you have lost nothing. But you lose everything if you meet Jesus and forget Him.

Thank you again for letting me share this glimpse with you. I am humbled by all of this. I hope there will be more to come as my journey continues. May the Lord bless you and keep you.

In Christ,
Debbie

Acknowledgments

I can't write this without thanking some very important people in my life. Thank you to Diane Dennis and Dawn Hankins for their help with editing and proofreading. But most importantly, Diane, you are such a faithful follower of our Lord and you have been such a support to me. I count it a privilege to call you my friend. Dawn, you know how much you and your family mean to me. Having your constant and loyal friendship has been one of my truest blessings from God. Love you, my dear friend.

Thank you to the people at WestBow for all your guidance, help, and encouragement. Thank you, Jan and Dale Marcum, for allowing me to share the mission field with you. Your work ethic and Christian example is amazing. I love you guys. Thank you, Tony and Pam Falcione, for giving me your love and friendship over the many years. Thank you to my friends at Family of Faith and Sisters in Christ (SIC) prayer breakfast group for supporting me. Also thank you to my friends at work who have encouraged me.

To my cuz, Michael Connell, thank you for always being here for me. We had so many great times growing up, especially with Jeannie and Buddy. I miss them both very much. Thank you, thank you for all the talks; you are a great listener and an even better friend.

Dad and Mom, Aubrey and Jewell Crickenberger, thank you both for making your faith real to me. Even in times of struggle, I knew your faith was real. Thanks, Dad, for instilling in me the desire to get into the Word of God on my own. I've watched you do it for years and would not have wanted anyone else to give me scriptural editing. Thanks, Mom, for being my mom, my best friend, and my *biggest* cheerleader. You have always believed in me. Words cannot describe how much I love you. Crystal, my sweet sister, I thank God for you. He has used you to open my eyes to much. Sissy loves you very much.

To Jared, Jason, Ashley, Jackson, and Addison; God blessed me as a mom with two terrific and remarkable sons. I really mean that—I love you both with all my heart. I know I was not always the most perfect mom, but I hope you know my love and support has and always will be there for you both. He added to that blessing a wonderful daughter-in-law, Ashley, whom I love as well, and then topped it off with the greatest grandchildren in the world, Jackson and Addison. GamMa Debbie loves you both!

Thank you to Karan Bingham for the powerful photo for the book cover. Your photos are breathtaking. I consider it an honor to use one of your photos my friend.

Thank you to Jared, my son, for the photos in the book. You captured in picture what I hope I captured in print. They made the book.

I will be a Father to you, and you will be my sons and daughters, says the Lord Almighty.

—2 Corinthians 6:18 NIV

Part 1

God, the Father

He Is Our Father

> I will be a Father to you, and you will be my sons and daughters, says the Lord Almighty.
> —2 Corinthians 6:18 NIV

> yet for us there is but one God, the Father, from whom all things came and for whom we live; and there is but one Lord, Jesus Christ, through whom all things came and through whom we live.
> —1 Corinthians 8:6 NIV

There is more to being a father than just having the name. Think of the things that make a good father. He loves you all the time, even when you do something wrong. A good father might correct you, but it's a fair correction based on his love for you. You might not agree at the time and think it unfair, but if you really thought honestly about it, you would see he was right.

A good father loves you enough to sometimes let you make your own decisions even though he knows it may be a mistake. And he is there to help you through the mistake. Sometimes, he helps you fix your mistakes. Sometimes, he is just there to be with you. He takes care of your scrapes and bruises and holds you while you cry.

Sounds like the qualities of both a good mother and father. That is our heavenly Father. He portrays everything good in both a mom and a dad. He loves us when we blame Him for all the bad things that happen and when we thank Him for all the good things that happen. His love never fails even when we call Him names or forget He even exists.

> Yet, O Lord, You are our Father; we are the clay, and
> You our Potter, and we are all the work of Your hand.
> —Isaiah 64:8 AB

He loved us when He created us, as we grow and when we leave this life. He will continue to be there for us and let us know ever so gently that He loves us. *Now that is a Father. I am glad that He is that kind of Father to me.*

More Scriptures: Psalm 68:5; Proverbs 3:11–12; Malachi 2:10; Matthew 5:16

Take Action: *If you want to have a Father who will never stop loving you, meet God the Father today. He is always waiting for His child.*

Prayer Requests/Answers:
_____
_____
_____
_____

He Is Ultimate Love

(written October 2001)

> For God so loved the world that he gave his one and only Son, that whoever believes in him shall not perish but have eternal life.
> —John 3:16 NIV

I woke up in the middle of the night with all these thoughts of God running through my mind. I grabbed some paper and pen, went into another room, and started writing word for word these thoughts. I don't know if these were God's true words to Jesus, but I would like to think maybe, just maybe, I got a glimpse into God's heart. I don't think I've ever changed a word.

"I knew this day would come. We have prepared for it before the beginning of time. I cannot bear to see You there bruised and bleeding, but I love them so much. They are My children. I know they do not understand."

"I will forgive them no matter what they have done or who they have done it to. I will forgive them, but they must ask. I will comfort them when they are in pain, even when they don't care to know Me. I will heal their bodies with Your stripes. I will be their peace when everything around them is in chaos. All they have to do is ask. I will love them even when they curse My name and despise You."

"I know they will not understand all that happens and question why, but a day will come when I will answer all, for I love them so much. They are My children. You understand My love for them, for You love them too! *That is why you chose to hang there and die.*"

"Someday they will understand. Until then, as always I will love them with an everlasting love."

> I have loved you with an everlasting love; Therefore
> I have drawn you with lovingkindness.
> —Jeremiah 31:3 NASB

More Scriptures: Romans 5:8; 1 John 3:1; 4:9

Take Action: He is waiting for you to ask. *Just ask!*

Prayer Requests/Answers:
_____
_____
_____
_____

He Forgives

> If my people, which are called by my name, shall humble themselves, and pray, and seek my face, and turn from their wicked ways; then will I hear from heaven, and will forgive their sin, and will heal their land.
>
> —2 Chronicles 7:14 KJV

When my children were younger, they still enjoyed when I would put them to bed at night. I would scratch their backs while I sang them a song; then we would say our prayers and I would kiss them good night. It didn't happen every night, but when it did, I think I enjoyed it more than they did because I knew there would come a day when it would stop (they would be too mature).

One such night I came into my younger son's room to tuck him in. With tear-filled eyes he proceeded to tell me that he had been lying there thinking about all the bad things he had done (he was only eight) and he was really sorry. I gathered him up in my arms and told him how much I appreciated him telling me this. And I wanted him to know that when he tells me he's sorry about those things, they're gone forever. And I told him that's what God does too. When we ask for forgiveness, He forgives and forgets.

Sometimes I don't feel qualified to talk to others about God. As a Christian, I've been hypocritical in the past and I'm sure I'll be in the future. I have said and done things that I know have saddened God. I think about all those things and I say the same thing to God that my son said to me. And my heavenly Father gathers me in His loving arms and tells me a story: "For God so loved the world that he gave his one and only Son, that whoever believes in him shall not perish but have eternal life" (John 3:16 NIV). What a wonderful story.

A Christian is merely a forgiven sinner who has made peace with God. We know it and choose that complete forgiveness that our heavenly Father holds in the nail-scarred hands of His Son, Jesus Christ, and by that act transforms us into children and saints of God. A non-Christian is simply an unforgiven sinner who had not made peace with God. They either don't know the Father or just don't yet want to. The Father's act of forgiveness is always there. He is waiting for each of us to come to Him, like my son came to me. *We* can choose, like my son, to tell the Father we are sorry and then accept that forgiveness He's been waiting to give. But we *must* choose. *Do not* delay any longer.

> You are kind and forgiving, O Lord, abounding in love to all who call to you.
> —Psalm 86:5 NIV

More Scriptures: Psalm 78:38; Daniel 9:9

Take Action: *When you go to bed tonight, let God tuck you in. Talk to Him; He will listen. Ask. He will forgive and forget.*

Prayer Requests/Answers:
_____
_____
_____
_____

He Is Our Boss

(written in 1999)

> And whatsoever ye do, do it heartily, as to the Lord, and not unto men; Knowing that of the Lord ye shall receive the reward of the inheritance: for ye serve the Lord Christ.
> —Colossians 3:23–24 KJV

Sounds pretty strange: God, the Employer. But isn't it true? We serve God, and because we serve God, we serve each other.

I have a friend I work with who has a sign that says "Who do you work for?" right on her desk. When she gets frustrated with the job or the situation around her, she looks at the sign and it reminds her that she is where she is because God wants her there to do His work.

A while ago I was struggling with work. I love the people I work with, but I felt I was drowning in all the endless paperwork. It was constantly changing, there was no satisfaction, and I felt as if my job had no meaning. I prayed that God would get me out of it.

Well, I'm still in the same job. I have prayed that God might send me somewhere else, but until then I work for Him right where I stand. Before I put my feet on the floor each morning, I try to thank Him for what the day will bring. But I've also been praying that if it is His desire for me to stay that He will change my desire to leave. Psalm 37:4 says, "Take delight in the Lord and he will give you the desires of your heart" (NIV). The more I come to know God, the more I realize the desires of my heart must come in sync with God's desires. If I am delighting in God, then my desire is that I am where He wants me to be. I'm not saying that my attitude is perfect every day. I have found, though, that I struggle less because I know that God desires the best for me. I also know the times I do struggle are when I put my desires first. I am here because He wants me here to do the best job for Him.

And you know He's got the best benefit package *(Romans 6:23—eternal life)* and retirement plan around *(John 14:2—many mansions)*.

> Seek first His kingdom.
> —Matthew 6:33 NASB

More Scriptures: Ephesians 6:6–7

Take Action: *So when you go to work today, see God in all that you do and do it with your whole heart for Him—no matter if you dig ditches, clean houses, work in a factory, work in a business, or watch children—because we have the best Boss in the world. He deserves our best effort.*

Prayer Request/Answers:
_____
_____
_____
_____

He Is the Healer of Our Soul

> He healeth the broken in heart, and bindeth up their wounds.
>
> —Psalm 147:3 KJV

I know the first questions that come to mind: Can we really call God a healer? Why does He choose to heal this person and not that one? I honestly do not know and I have wondered about these same questions.

I can tell you, though, that when I allow myself to take my eyes off God and put them on the situation, that is when the questions flood in and the peace I once had is overwhelmed. Those situations that are beyond my comprehension to ever understand, I give to God to get me through. Sometimes I do well at that; sometimes I don't.

I think sometimes we forget the eternity of God. He is an eternal spirit (John 4:24) and because He is a spirit, He looks at the parts of us that are most important, that essence of life that He breathed into each of us, our spirit (heart) and soul. He holds dear the part that communes with Him on a level that most of us will never be able to describe in mere human terms, or if we were truly honest, could ever really deny it exists. In a world where you can change the color of your hair, eyes, and other physical parts, He seeks the part of us that will forever be truly us and always His, our spirit (heart) and soul.

He wants to heal our heart and soul in such a way that even in the deepest despair of human tragedy or adverse circumstances of life, we can triumph and be a living testimony to His grace, mercy, compassion, and strength. If you ever read another book in your life, make it *The Hiding Place* by Corrie ten Boom. I've read it at least three times, and I guess I finally got it. Corrie's family was arrested and imprisoned during World War II for helping Jews. Through the torturous events of her imprisonment, including the death of some of her family members, she overcame the hate she felt for her captors'. She did this by allowing the God of grace and mercy to heal her in a way she could not do on her own. And because of that healing she was able to forgive and even come to love the ones who had abused her and killed her family.

Only the God who loved her, and us, so much that He willing gave His Son, Jesus, as the price for our atonement could heal her heart in this way. Only the God who because of His great love and mercy for us (John 3:16), could watch His Son be ridiculed, falsely accused, beaten, and die horrifically on the cross (Isaiah 53:5, I Peter 2:24; Luke 23:34), and yet extend forgiveness, mercy and love to those who committed those acts (all of us).

Only our God is able to heal hearts as He did Corrie's. He is waiting with open arms to heal any heart that is willing. Are you willing to give Him that chance?

More Scriptures: Psalm 32:7; 40:2; 41:4; 42; 43; 119:114; Isaiah 32:2; Jeremiah 31:2

Take Action: *Psalm 43:4 says, "Then will I go unto the altar of God" (KJV). Go to God right now and in His strength you will find healing in your heart for anything and everything you need.*

Prayer Requests/Answers:

_____
_____
_____
_____

He Is the Alpha and the Omega—the Beginning and the End

> I am Alpha and Omega, the beginning and the ending, saith the Lord, which is, and which was, and which is to come, the Almighty.
> —Revelation 1:8 KJV

Both my grandmothers were such neat ladies. My mom's mom, Ethel, died in her eighties. She lived a long life, experiencing incredible events in history and seeing amazing inventions during her time. She used to tell me how life was when she was growing up. She could remember the old Model T cars when they first appeared on the scene. She experienced life during all the great wars of our century. The computer age was just getting started when she passed away. Now I am the one to pass on the stories of how life was in the sixties and seventies to my children. Of course, they sometimes laugh at those stories about how dorky things were (well, okay, maybe it was how dorky I was). But they, too, will someday tell their children about how life was like when they were growing up.

But God, the Alpha—the beginning—was there at creation (Psalm 90:2). He was there when you were born and will be there when you die. He's been there during all the wars that men have started to try to prove their greatness. He has watched people show great human kindness to their fellow man and He has seen them cause unspeakable pain.

Still, He watches over all of us, giving each one chance after chance to seek Him out (2 Peter 3:9). And maybe because He knows what the future holds, God, the Omega—the end—does continue to give us those chances time after time to come to Him.

> This is what the LORD says—Israel's King and Redeemer, the LORD Almighty: I am the first and I am the last; apart from me there is no God.
> —Isaiah 44:6 NIV

More Scriptures: Isaiah 41:4; Revelation 1:17

Take Action: <u>Begin</u> *today to learn of God and love God and hold on to Him until the* <u>end</u>.

Prayer Requests/Answers:

_____
_____
_____
_____

He Is Our Refuge and Strength

> God is our refuge and strength, a very present help in trouble.
>
> —Psalm 46:1 KJV

Life can be a struggle. And it's not always because of the major things that happen (accidents, illness, and death). It is the constant, everyday things that sometimes seem to wear us down the most. Work, family disagreements, cleaning the house and yard, grocery shopping, and bills are just some things that can take the joy right out of our souls. Well, at least, sometimes they sure take my joy away.

So this is what I have learned to do at times like those. When you feel that the joy is gone, check yourself. Where is your eye level? Is it staring at the problem? If it is, do some adjusting. Look up to God's level. He's above it all. He sees the end, so trust in Him to carry you through, not necessarily to get you out of it: "The eternal God is *thy* refuge, and underneath *are* the everlasting arms:" (Deuteronomy 33:27 KJV). He has His strong arms underneath ours to carry us through no matter how *BIG* or how *small* the situation seems.

"He that dwelleth in the secret place of the most High shall abide under the shadow of the Almighty" (Psalm 91:1 KJV). What a promise He gives us. We live with the most high God and we can rest under His shadow. He will be our strength. He always has room for one more.

> But the Lord is my defense; and my God is the rock of my refuge.
>
> —Psalm 94:22 KJV

Debra Niswander

More Scriptures: Psalm 9:9; 57:1; 59:16; 62:7

Take Action: *Go to the spiritual eye doctor and He will teach you to focus on the things above and not on the things below.*

Prayer Requests/Answers:
_____
_____
_____
_____

He Is the Peacemaker

(written August 2000)

Thou wilt keep *him* in perfect peace, *whose* mind *is* stayed *on thee:* because he trusteth in thee.
—Isaiah 26:3 KJV

The mind is a funny thing. And who has really figured it out? We see all of man's intelligence—we can get a man to the moon, we have made advances in medicine that have enhanced our lives, and now we seem to be even close to cracking all the mysteries of the code of life. But the mind: what do we really know?

We seem to have come a long way with psychology and mental disorders. But have we really? What are people really thinking and why? What makes a person walk into a building and begin shooting unarmed, innocent people; or what causes a man to one day be walking down Wall Street in a pin-striped suit, and the next to be living in a cardboard box? What drives each of us to do the things we do? And what drives a man who you know loves the Lord with all his heart and soul, but whose mind can't seem to grasp that same love, to one day take his life?

For all our intelligence, we can let our minds talk us into doing the most stupid things, even when in our hearts we know it's wrong. In our hearts we know God loves us, but we talk ourselves out of it or we let Satan do it for us. In our hearts we know of His promise of peace, but we just won't let the mind accept that as the answer. We think sometimes God let us down because the answers we got weren't the answers we wanted.

God says *He* will keep us in perfect peace whose mind is stayed on Him. The Bible doesn't say He'll give us the answers we want to all our questions. It says something much better: He'll give us the peace it takes to handle whatever the question is. In our minds we may never have the answers, but we'll have the peace because our minds are not focusing on the questions, but on God Himself. And we are also told that if we would focus on God, that although outwardly circumstances may stay the same, inwardly we change—because His peace is perfect. That means it settles all the questions in our minds. We must let Him be our peace, and only then can His perfect peace become ours. Then maybe we won't worry so much if we don't get the answers we want to hear.

> And the peace of God, which transcends all understanding, will guard your hearts and your minds in Christ Jesus.
> —Philippians 4:7 NIV

More Scriptures: Proverbs 3:5; John 16:35; 2 Timothy 1:7

Take Action: *When the war of questions comes—and they will—let God fight the battles with His perfect weapon: <u>Himself</u>. He is our peace, our hope, our salvation, our victory.*

Prayer Requests/Answers:

_____
_____
_____
_____

He Is THE Answer

> And therefore will the Lord wait, that he may be gracious unto you, and therefore will he be exalted, that he may have mercy upon you: for the Lord is a God of judgment: blessed *are* all they that wait for him.
>
> —Isaiah 30:18 KJV

My life is not a complicated one. I have complicated it by my choice of priorities. I try to fill each day with so many busy "things to do" that many days I miss the most important thing for that day: to meet with God and enjoy another day as His child.

Oh, I give Him a few minutes, sometimes, in the morning to read a little and pray those quick thoughts: "Help me to do Your will today." "Be with me and my family and friends today." But, I realized I truly don't talk to Him and say to Him, "What is it You want me to do today?" I don't really wait for Him to answer. I scurry about trying to meet the deadlines I have placed on myself and others have placed on me today. I never ask Him what His deadline is for me today. I truly can't take one day at a time (Matthew 6:34), because I've placed so many "things" in my schedule, I'm always looking at least a week ahead to try to stay ahead. I don't know the meaning of the words "caught up."

So I am here at four o'clock in the morning, finding that God is all the things He says He is in Isaiah 30:18. He longs to be gracious to me and He rises to show me compassion. In Him I find the rest I need; He quiets my soul. In Him I trust and find strength, and because of that, I'm finding in Him I have all the answers I need to make each day complete, no matter what the day holds.

> Call to Me and I will answer you, and show you great and mighty things, which you do not know.
> —Jeremiah 33:3 NKJV

More Scriptures: Job 13:22; Psalm 91:15; Isaiah 58:9–11

Take Action: *When you're looking for the answers, consider where the questions come from. Maybe it was from the one who's always had the answers. He's just been waiting for you to ask.*

Prayer Requests/Answers:
_____
_____
_____
_____

I AM

And Moses said unto God, Behold, *when* I come unto the children of Israel, and shall say unto them, The God of your fathers hath sent me unto you; and they shall say to me, What *is* his name? What shall I say unto them? And God said unto Moses, I AM THAT I AM: and he said, Thus shalt thou say unto the children of Israel, I AM hath sent me unto you.
—Exodus 3:13–14 KJV

Jesus said unto them, Verily, verily, I say unto you, Before Abraham was, I am.
—John 8:58 KJV

You are the Creator?—I AM
You are the creator of me?—I AM
You are the protector of my soul?—I AM
You are peace in the midst of turmoil?—I AM
You are comfort when nothing else will do?—I AM
You are healing, inside and out?—I AM
You are mercy and grace?—I AM
You are freedom?—I AM
You are life?—I AM
You are truth?—I AM
You are the true lover of my soul?—I AM

Probably the most significant revelation each of us must face is that it is not what God gives us or does for us, but God Himself and what He alone embodies is all we need and what we must want and hope to have. That in Him and in Him alone, we have our existence (Acts 17:28). And in that revelation, we realize that only by Him and through Him can we obtain the true greatness He desires for us and essentially what we want for ourselves.

Until we relinquish our control and dependence on all else—including our own abilities to achieve success—and rely on Him, it is certain that at some point we will run right smack into disappointment or failure. When the expectations of what *we think* our lives should be meets what they really are, *then we see* what they could be by and through Him. Once there, we finally yield to the desires of what the great I AM has planned for our lives and we realize true happiness, peace, and contentment. It is in those moments when all is stripped away and the great I AM stands before us as our source for all things, that we can see that *He and only He* is enough and that nothing and no one else can come close.

How do I know? I've been there a time or two. That is when the words of Job ring the truest: "Naked I came from my mother's womb, and naked I will depart. The LORD gave and the LORD has taken away; may the name of the LORD be praised" (Job 1:21 NIV).

More Scriptures: Exodus 6:2–3; Psalm 83:18; Colossians 1:17; Revelation 1:8

Take Action: *You are enough for me! I AM.*

Prayer Requests/Answers:
_____
_____
_____
_____

This is how God showed his love among us: He sent his one and only Son into the world that we might live through him.

—1 John 4:9 NIV

Part 2

God, the Son

Jesus: A Love Story

> "Ever since the time of your forefathers you have turned away from my decrees and have not kept them. Return to me and I will return to you," says the LORD Almighty. "But you ask, 'How are we to return?'"
>
> —Malachi 3:7 NIV

> This is love: not that we loved God, but that he loved us and sent his Son as an atoning sacrifice for our sins.
> —1 John 4:10 NIV

The Holy Bible is such an interesting book. It tells the history of a group of people and their journey through life. Some of it is not very flattering. But I think if each of us were to have our own history written, we would all have some moments we would just as soon end up on the editing room floor. (I know I would have more than I would like to admit.) However, the Bible is something so much more, because woven throughout that history is a love story. It is a love story that is truly like no other one, one by which all others pale in comparison. And what's more, it is a love story not just for a select few, but for all of mankind—including me, including you.

It is the story of a Creator who breathed life into His beloved creation: man (Genesis 2:7). He made him unlike any other creation before or after. With the breath of God, man became a living soul, created in the image and likeness of the Creator (Genesis 1:26).

This love story reveals the lengths our Creator went through to demonstrate His love for His most cherished creation. It is a love so intense that our Creator, even after countless acts of rejection (Romans 5:8) still sacrificed His only Son—the only one He loved more than man—to show us what true love looks like. It is in the shape of a *cross*.

> I pray that out of his glorious riches he may strengthen you with power through his Spirit in your inner being, so that Christ may dwell in your hearts through faith. And I pray that you, being rooted and established in love, may have power, together with all the saints, to grasp how wide and long and high and deep is the love of Christ,
> —Ephesians 3:16–18 NIV

More Scriptures: John 15:13; Romans 8:38–39; 1 John 3:16

Take Action: *And we shall live happily ever after.*

Prayer Requests/Answers:
_____
_____
_____
_____

Jesus: The Son's Love for His Father; the Son's Love for Us

> but the world must learn that I love the Father and that I do exactly what my Father has commanded me. Come now; let us leave.
>
> —John 14:31 NIV

I can't imagine the emptiness Jesus must have felt knowing His Father could not look at Him because of our sin that now laid upon His shoulders. I wonder if these might be the words He wanted to say:

"Father, why won't You look at Me? Why have You turned Your back?

"They mock Me; they curse You. Most of the time, they deny You even exist to justify the choices in their lives. In the middle of the night, they wonder why the fear they hide during the day cannot be extinguished. They wonder why all the material things they have gained, their money, possessions, or power, cannot bring them peace.

"But, Father, I love them as You love them. I understand My choice. We have chosen this place in time to give them the way back. I could choose to say no, but that would mean eternal death for all of them and I cannot bear that" (see Psalm 102:19–20).

"So, I ask of You, Father, to forgive them, for they do not yet understand. Someday each one will. That if they only ask, I can change their lives. I can give them more than a mere existence in a temporary world. I can replace their fear with love that never fails (see Romans 8:39), their loneliness with peace that passes all understanding (see Philippines 4:7), and I will give them a hope that goes beyond this world to the next (see John 14:1–2). And if they ask, We will welcome them with outstretched arms. My heart smiles when I hear them ask.

"Father, there is nothing left to do, but to show Our love for them. It is finished."

"With that, he bowed his head and gave up his spirit" (John 19:30 NIV).

> The Father loves me because I give my life so that I can take it back again. No one takes it away from me; I give my own life freely. I have the right to give my life, and I have the right to take it back. This is what my Father commanded me to do.
> —John 10:17–18 NCV

More Scriptures: 1 John 4:9–10; Revelation 3:20

Take Action: *Jesus' love for you was more important than His life to Him. Ask and see His heart smile!*

Prayer Requests/Answers:
_____
_____
_____
_____

Jesus: The Giver of Second Chances, and Third Chances, and Fourth Chances, and …

> My dear children, I write this to you so that you will not sin. But if anybody does sin, we have one who speaks to the Father in our defense — Jesus Christ, the Righteous One. He is the atoning sacrifice for our sins, and not only for ours but also for the sins of the whole world.
>
> —1 John 2:1–2 NIV

"I tell you the truth," Jesus answered, "this very night, before the rooster crows, you will disown me three times." But Peter declared, "Even if I have to die with you, I will never disown you." And all the other disciples said the same —Matthew 26:34–35 NIV. I think when Peter said that to Jesus, he meant that with all his heart. I don't think he ever thought he would put himself in a position where he would deny Christ, much less actually do it. But he did.

Have you ever done that? I have. I've thought to myself (or even said it out loud), "I would never act like that" or "You'll never catch me doing that." "That" meaning putting myself in a position to commit a sin, and in so doing, deny Christ. And what happened? I actually did, just like Peter.

I often wonder why this particular story is told. I wonder how Peter must have felt when he realized he had failed Jesus. See, Peter had been in the presence of Jesus, he sat at His feet, listened to His preaching, and even after all that, when a true test came along, he failed miserably. Scripture says he wept bitterly. I've known that feeling. I know the presence of Jesus. I know Him as Savior, I read His Word, and still sometimes when a real test presents itself, I fail miserably. I've wept bitterly.

I think Peter's story was written for me, because even though Peter failed Jesus, Jesus didn't fail Peter. He gave Peter a second chance (probably a third, and a fourth, and more). Scripture doesn't specifically tell us of any exchange between Peter and Jesus about his denial, but for Jesus (after His resurrection) to command Peter to feed His sheep (John 21:15–17) tells me that Jesus gave Peter another chance. And we all know that Peter took that command and proclaimed the saving grace of Jesus to the world.

I can tell you about my exchanges with Jesus when I have failed. He doesn't fail me. I can sum it up with Lamentations 3:22–23: "It is of the Lord's mercies that we are not consumed, because his compassions fail not. *They are* new every morning: great is thy faithfulness" (KJV). I thank Him for giving me a second chance (and yes, a third, and a fourth, and more). I too want to proclaim His saving grace to the world.

> The LORD appeared to us in the past, saying: "I have loved you with an everlasting love; I have drawn you with loving-kindness.
> —Jeremiah 31:3 NIV

More Scriptures: Psalm 103:11–12; Malachi 3:6–7

Take Action: *Maybe you realize Peter's story was written for you too. Let Jesus give you a second chance (and maybe more) and proclaim with me His saving grace.*

Prayer Requests/Answers:
_____
_____
_____
_____

Jesus: Our Freedom Fighter

> "The Spirit of the Lord is on me, because he has anointed me to preach good news to the poor. He has sent me to *proclaim freedom for the prisoners* and recovery of sight for the blind, to release the oppressed, to proclaim the year of the Lord's favor."
> —Luke 4:18–19 NIV (emphasis mine)

Jesus declares in this Scripture that He has come to set the captives free. The captives are us. The freedom is from everything that chains us to a life without Him.

First and foremost, He freed us from sin (spiritual death) by becoming the ultimate sacrifice and paying the price for our sin. Only a perfect sacrifice could make us right with God (Isaiah 53:4–6). Second Corinthians 5:21 (NIV) tells us, "God made him who had no sin to be sin for us, so that in him we might become the righteousness of God." He then freed us from the fear of physical death itself by raising Himself from the dead (Romans 6:9; 10:9). "I am the Living One; I was dead, and behold I am alive for ever and ever! And I hold the keys of death and Hades" (Revelation 1:18 NIV).

He also freed us from the chains we place on ourselves. You know some of them; maybe you only have one, maybe more, but you know them—fears that hold you back, baggage you carry from past hurts or failures. Maybe you feel you've had one trial or tribulation too many. Maybe you have already experienced the first freedom Jesus gives when you received His saving grace, but those other chains still keep dragging you down. So what do you do?

Start with what I've been trying to do: stop picking the chains back up when Jesus unlocks them. Paul didn't miss any in Romans

8:35–39, declaring that nothing shall separate us from His love—even the chains we still keep holding on to. "For we do not have a high priest who is unable to sympathize with our weaknesses, but we have one who has been tempted in every way, just as we are—yet was without sin" (Hebrews 4:15 NIV). He understands what all those chains are like. We have a God, the only God, who understands our fears, knows of our baggage, and has been there through the trials and tribulations, and He is the only one able to cast off those chains for good! He is the key that unlocked them for us once and for all. We don't have to keep taking them back. Jesus said it Himself in John 8:36, "So if the Son sets you free, you will be free indeed" (NIV).

> Jesus said to her, "I am the resurrection and the life.
> He who believes in me will live, even though he dies;
> and whoever lives and believes in me will never die.
> Do you believe this?
> —John 11:25–26 NIV

More Scriptures: Psalm 118:5; Isaiah 42:1–8; 58:6; 61:1; John 8:31–33

Take Action: *So drop the chains and <u>claim the words</u> of Paul in Romans 8:37: "No, in all these things we are more than <u>conquerors through him</u> who loved us" (NIV, emphasis mine).*

Prayer Requests/Answers:
_____
_____
_____

Jesus: His Scars, Our Healing

> Now Thomas (called Didymus), one of the Twelve, was not with the disciples when Jesus came. When the other disciples told him that they had seen the Lord, he declared, "Unless I see the nail marks in his hands and put my finger where the nails were, and put my hand into his side, I will not believe it." A week later his disciples were in the house again, and Thomas was with them. Though the doors were locked, Jesus came and stood among them and said, "Peace be with you!" Then he said to Thomas, "Put your finger here; see my hands. Reach out your hand and put it into my side. Stop doubting and believe." Thomas said to him, "My Lord and my God!"
> —John 20:24–28 NIV

I thought it was very interesting that Thomas wanted to see the scars of Jesus' wounds. He didn't want to see His face or look in His eyes. For Thomas, the marks from the wounds were the proof. Maybe they were the testimony to Thomas that Jesus was indeed Lord, that all Jesus had said He was and all He would do were reflected in those scars.

I got to thinking about those scars. Why do some wounds, when they heal, leave nothing behind? You would never know they were there. Others leave marks that over time actually fade and become hardly noticeable. We soon forget them and only occasionally by seeing or feeling the remnant are we reminded of the incident that caused the wound and the pain that came with it. Most of the time we don't seem to dwell on it; we've moved on. It has healed.

But there are some scars that are so deep they never go away. Some even disfigure. They are a constant reminder to us of the pain we suffered and that healing never truly came. And I don't just mean physical scars. The emotional and mental scars that go with a wound like that can be even more traumatic. Or maybe the wounds we have suffered don't leave outward scars but have left deep and lasting marks on our hearts and souls.

> But he was pierced for our transgressions, he was crushed for our iniquities; the punishment that brought us peace was upon him, and by his wounds we are healed.
> —Isaiah 53:5 NIV

Look at Jesus' scars one more time. Really look at them. They are there to remind us, to show us, that because He wears scars, we don't have to. The wounds we have are healed through Him. No matter how deep they are, no matter how old they are, no matter how disfigured they have become, He can heal them to where there is nothing left behind. They can become just a faint memory.

> O Lord my God, I cried unto thee, and thou has healed me.
> —Psalm 30:2 KJV

More Scriptures: Psalm 103:1–4

Take Action: *Take His hand; touch His side. Let Him heal your wound and remove the scar.*

Prayer Requests/Answers:

_____
_____
_____
_____

Jesus: Was, Is, and Always Will Be

> Jesus Christ is the same yesterday and today and forever.
>
> —Hebrews 13:8 NIV

When Jesus walked the earth, He brought freedom, healing, and life to people. He came into their lives and met them in their need and fulfilled it. People were healed from their diseases and some were even raised from the dead. People living with fears and burdens were freed. Hope was restored. Salvation was given. Jesus brought them back to God.

If you believe the above verse, if you believe who Christ is, then you must realize that the power He demonstrated while on earth didn't end. That power continues today. His power didn't start or end on the cross (Hebrews 1:10–12).

Sickness and disease haven't changed; they still cripple our bodies, minds, and spirits. Death means you still die. The anger, grief, and struggles of life sometimes still leave us helpless and hopeless. Sin was sin then and it remains sin now. But if the power of *Christ* could heal then, it still heals now. The power that raised lifeless bodies then, does that now. If Christ could give a glimpse of hope back to someone who had all but lost it then, He most certainly does that now. Christ offered forgiveness and salvation then, and He offers it now. Christ still brings us back to God. "Lift up your eyes to the heavens, look at the earth beneath; the heavens will vanish like smoke, the earth will wear out like a garment and it inhabitants die like flies. But my salvation will last forever, my righteousness will never fail" (Isaiah 51:6 NIV).

Nothing has changed when it comes to Christ's power, or when it comes to Christ Himself: "For I *am* the Lord, I change not" (Malachi 3:6 KJV). He touches our bodies, souls, and spirits now as He did then. He is timeless and limitless. As Christ Himself says, "Heaven and earth will pass away, but my words will never pass away" (Matthew 24:35; Mark 13:31; Luke 21:33 NIV).

More Scriptures: Numbers 23:19; Psalm 102:25–27; John 8:58; James 1:17

Take Action: *What He did for those then, He will do for you now. Let Him bring you back to God!*

Prayer Requests/Answers:
_____
_____
_____
_____

Do You Know the Word of God (the Bible) and the Word (Jesus)?

> In the beginning was the Word, and the Word was with God, and the Word was God. He was with God in the beginning. Through him all things were made; without him nothing was made that has been made.
> —John 1:1–3 NIV

In high school I had an English teacher who loved to pick on me. He found out one day in a class discussion that I believed in the Bible, and after that it became a nearly everyday occurrence for him to see how he could embarrass me. In this particular class, we discussed literary works and he thought it was ridiculous that I thought the Bible to be true. You see, he had read the Bible and probably knew it better than I did—well, I should say that he could quote passages better than I could. He knew the Word of God (the Bible), but he did not know the Word (Jesus). To him the Bible was a fascinating literary work, but that was all.

I actually felt sorry for him. For all his intelligence (and he really was smart), he was blind to the knowledge that the Word of God was about Jesus—the Word: "But the natural man does not receive the things of the Spirit of God, for they are foolishness to him; nor can he know *them*, because they are spiritually discerned" (1 Corinthians 2:14 NKJV). When reading the Word, you must forget what you think you know; you must look past your human viewpoint and see through your spirit, and when you do, God will reveal Himself to you.

> The Word became flesh and lived for a while among us. We have seen his glory, the glory of the one and only Son, who came from the Father, full of grace and truth.
> —John 1:14 NIV

Jesus Himself said, "The thief cometh not, but for to steal, and to kill, and to destroy: I am come that they might have life, and that they might have it more abundantly" (John 10:10 KJV).

If you let Him, He will open up your blinded eyes (Psalm 146:8) so that when you look at the pages of the Bible, instead of where you once only saw words, you now see the Word, who is Jesus, and that in Jesus you see life: "In him was life, and that life was the light of men" (John 1:4 NIV).

> This is how God showed his love among us: He sent his one and only Son into the world that we might live through him.
> —1 John 4:9 NIV

More Scriptures: John 11:25; 1 John 1:2

Take Action: *Read the Word of God and ask God to let you see the "Word" of God. Jesus is the only Word that truly gives you life in <u>His</u> words.*

Prayer Requests/Answers:
_____
_____
_____
_____

Jesus: The Master Painter

> For you have been born again, not of perishable seed, but of imperishable, through the living and enduring word of God.
>
> —1 Peter 1:23 NIV

The pastor at my church began a series called "Who Am I in Christ?" He gave different people in our congregation Scripture verses and asked us to describe how the verse related to us in terms of the question in the series. Mine was the verse above. I shared my experiences of the two questions that most people ask when they hear the phrase "born again." They are, What do you mean by "born again"? and How do you know you're born again?

In describing my experiences, I gave my testimony of how I met Jesus Christ when I was ten years old. This was my answer to the question, How do I know I am born again? (see the devotional under "Faith": "I Know That I Know That I Know", page 153). In answering the other question (What do you mean "born again"?), I described it as follows:

> I have a painting that has colors all over it. (Well, most people wouldn't consider it a painting.) The painting is *really, really* bad. I don't have my older son's artistic side or my younger son's woodworking ability, but this is the best way to illustrate what I was and am without Christ: chaotic, disorganized in thought and direction, nothing good, no beauty. Literally, I was a mess inside (just like the painting). This painting could reflect each of us without Christ.
>
> We try to paint over the mess, to fix ourselves, to show we are a good person to others and to ourselves. We use a

combination of paints and an assortment of colors. Some of us use no technique at all and cover the mess with even more mess: drugs, alcohol, or an abusive lifestyle. Some of us study and we use vibrant colors and develop specific techniques or lifestyles like education, career, possessions, or wealth to cover up the mess and (sometimes) portray a great picture on the surface. But underneath the painting we have created, the mess still remains.

Then there comes a day when we meet the Master Painter. There is only one color He uses and only one color He needs: bright red. Once it touches the canvas of a life, it transforms the messy colors to white, white as snow: "Come now, let us reason together," says the Lord. "Though your sins are like scarlet, they shall be white as snow; though they are red as crimson, they shall be like wool" (Isaiah 1:18 NIV). With one stroke of His brush, He changes the chaos and mess to perfect beauty that rivals any painting ever created. A brush that was fashioned from a cross where once we were bound by sin, we are now set free; once tormented by guilt and shame, now restored by grace; once lost, now found; once hindered by disease, now healed by His stripes; once without direction, now led by His Spirit; once loving only self, now loving others; once dead, now alive; once without hope, now a future here but also to come.

He takes our mess and He makes us a masterpiece.

Therefore if any man *be* in Christ, *he is* a new creature: old things are passed away; behold, all things are become new.
—2 Corinthians 5:17 KJV

A Glimpse of God

More Scriptures: Matthew 1:21; John 1:12–13; 3:3; Acts 4:12; 1 John 1:29

Take Action: *Put your brush down. Let Christ use His brush and make you a masterpiece.*

Prayer Requests/Answers:
_____
_____
_____
_____

Jesus: Our Savior

She will give birth to a son, and you are to give him the name Jesus, because he will save his people from their sins.
—Matthew 1:21 NIV

Salvation is found in no one else, for there is no other name under heaven given to men by which we must be saved.
—Acts 4:12 NIV

The band, Tenth Avenue North, has one of the best songs that describes what the cross of salvation means to the remaking of a person. It has become one of my favorite songs. It's called "You Are More." Part of the words in the song say ...

'Cause this is not about what you've done but what's been done for you.
This is not about where you've been but where your brokenness brings you to
This is not about what you feel, but what He felt to forgive you, and what He felt to make you loved.
You are more than the choices that you've made; You are more than the sum of your past mistakes,
You are more than the problems you create, You've been remade.
—Mike Donehey and Jason Ingram

The video is even more compelling. As they are singing there are scenes of people writing their sins, their failures, their fears, their hang-ups on a chalkboard. Then water starts running down the chalkboard and pretty soon the chalkboard is clean.

What did Christ do for you? He took away all the things that you (all of us) should be judged for and He remade you. And what did He remake you into? Himself. So when God looks at you, He sees His Son: pure, holy, blameless, perfection. Everything that Christ is, you are now: "Therefore, if any man be in Christ, *he is* a new creature: old things are passed away; behold, all things are become new" (2 Corinthians 5:17 KJV).

He saved you from yourself. He saved me from myself. Don't concentrate on your sins, your weaknesses, your failures, because if you know Jesus as your Savior, that is not who you are. They do not define you. And what you see as your accomplishments in no way defines you either. Jesus defines who you are. It is the blood of Christ that expunges our sins. When God the Father sees that blood on our hearts, He sees us pure and clean. Even though we may be a work in progress, He sees us as complete and perfect in Christ (Colossians 2:10). In Jesus you are forgiven, and a child of God. You are a new person; there is nothing there to be judged: "Therefore there is now no condemnation for those who are in Christ Jesus. For the law of the Spirit of life in Christ Jesus has set you free from the law of sin and death" (Romans 8:1–2 NASB).

Just like the water washed the chalkboard clean, that is what Jesus does for us. We have a clean slate: "as far as the east is from the west, so far has he removed our transgressions from us" (Psalm 103:12 NIV).

> I am not ashamed of the gospel, because it is the power of God for the salvation of everyone who believes: first for the Jew, then to the Gentile.
> —Romans 1:16 NIV

More Scriptures: Isaiah 43:11; Luke 19:10; John 3:17; 14:6

Take Action: *You can be remade no matter what you've done. Jesus, your Savior, remakes you. Let Him.*

Prayer Requests/Answers:
_____
_____
_____

Jesus: You Know Him as Savior; Do You Know Him as Lord?

> Then Jesus said to his disciples, "If anyone would come after me, he must deny himself and take up his cross and follow me.
> —Matthew 16:24 NIV

I must admit this has been an uncomfortable devotional for me to write. I certainly know Jesus as Savior and wholeheartedly believe He has forgiven me and made me right with God. Yet there are times when I can't say I make Him Lord. Not that I'm not trying. But I've come to understand Paul's urging to crucify ourselves daily, learning to surrender ourselves to His authority: "Therefore I urge you, brethren, by the mercies of God, to present your bodies a living and holy sacrifice, acceptable to God, *which is your spiritual service of worship*" (Romans 12:1 NASB).

That's the kicker. We certainly want to make Him Savior, but making Him Lord, well, that's another story. Or, okay, I'll make Him Lord when it comes to some of my money, some of my friends, certain parts of my life. But wait a minute, don't ask me for everything. Come on, I have a life here—I want to buy this; I want to go here; I want this job. I pay my tithes, go to church, volunteer. Sometimes though, I want to do my own thing in my own way. Well, that's me in a nutshell at times.

It's hard to think of the lordship of Jesus Christ. I think it might be because of the concept of the word *lord*. For someone to be lord over you means they have absolute control over you. They hold your life in their hands. You have no choice but to obey. But that is not the lordship of Jesus.

It is our choice to follow Him and call Him Lord. After what He did for us as Savior, it shouldn't be a hard choice. It should come from gratitude and love. That is certainly what He wants it to be, to obey out of love. But it's hard sometimes, because although we are saying to Him, "I give You authority over my life, my desires, my wants," we are afraid of what that means our lives will look like. (At least, I have had those thoughts) "I have been crucified with Christ and I no longer live, but Christ lives in me. The life I live in the body, I live by faith in the Son of God, who loved me and gave himself for me" (Galatians 2:20 NIV).

I think we get so caught up living the life that we see in our natural eyes, we forget about the life we can't see. We tend to believe that eternal life begins at death, but it really began the day we were conceived and became living souls! It is a life that God gives each of us, with plans beyond our imagination. The choice is ours as to which life we follow here on earth: one where we are lord or one where He is. It is hard to live a life that doesn't promote our own self-interest but promotes God's. But we might want to remember that although we might not make Him Lord here and now, there will be *no* doubt who is Lord in heaven: "Therefore God exalted him to the highest place and gave him the name that is above every name, that at the name of Jesus every knee should bow, in heaven and on earth and under the earth, and every tongue confess that Jesus Christ is Lord, to the glory of God the Father." (Philippians 2:9–11 NIV).

> yet for us there is but one God, the Father, from whom all things came and for whom we live; and there is but one Lord, Jesus Christ, through whom all things came and through whom we live.
> —1 Corinthians 8:6 NIV

A Glimpse of God

More Scriptures: Acts 2:36; Romans 14:9

Take Action: *Christ made a choice for us; let's make a choice for Him.*

Prayer Requests/Answers:
_____
_____
_____
_____

If anyone believes in me, rivers of living water will flow out from that person's heart, as the Scripture says.

—John 7:38 NCV

Part 3

God, the Holy Spirit

Truth's Voice

> When the Counselor comes, whom I will send to you from the Father, the Spirit of truth who goes out from the Father, he will testify about me.
> —John 15:26 NIV

Truth does have a voice. And when you hear Him and listen to what He says, your life will be changed. He is described as a counselor, a comforter, a helper, a teacher, a conqueror, and an intercessor, to name a few. You can hear His voice throughout the Word of God, but He also might come loudly like a rushing, mighty wind so as to drown out the other voices that keep you from enjoying what He offers. You might hear Him out loud or in your head. He might come in a word, in a song, through a person. Or He might come like a still, small voice, so quiet and soft that you let go of anything that distracts you for the chance to embrace what His voice brings.

However He comes, stop for a moment this time and listen, really listen, and you will hear echoes of love: "I have loved you with an everlasting love; Therefore I have drawn you with lovingkindness" (Jeremiah 31:3 NASB). Salvation flows from His voice: "For God so loved the world, that He gave His only begotten Son, that whoever believes in Him shall not perish, but have eternal life" (John 3:16 NASB). True freedom rings from His voice: "If the Son therefore shall make you free, ye shall be free indeed" (John 8:36 KJV). Eternal life comes to those who hear His voice: "For the wages of sin is death; but the gift of God is eternal life through Jesus Christ our Lord" (Romans 6:23 KJV).

He opens your eyes to the Word of God, where once it was as dry as the original parchments written upon to now where the words literally jump off the page and bring nourishment to your soul. He guides you to the Father, and you learn the truth of where your destiny lies: in and through Him (Psalm 16:5).

> But when he, the Spirit of truth, comes, he will guide you into all truth. He will not speak on his own; he will speak only what he hears, and he will tell you what is yet to come. He will bring glory to me by taking from what is mine and making it known to you. All that belongs to the Father is mine. That is why I said the Spirit will take from what is mine and make it known to you.
> —John 16:13–15 NIV

More Scriptures: John 14:17, 26; 16:7

Take Action: *Shhh ... listen. Don't you hear Him? He's talking to you. Just listen.*

Prayer Requests/Answers:
_____
_____
_____
_____

Signed, Sealed, and Delivered

> In Him you also who have heard the Word of Truth, the glad tidings (Gospel) of your salvation, and have believed in *and* adhered to *and* relied on Him, were stamped with the seal of the long-promised Holy Spirit.
> —Ephesians 1:13 (AB)

In my capacity as probate register, when I certify a document to be an exact copy of what the original file contains, I sign my name and place the state's seal on the document over my signature. The stamp embeds the seal into the document, and the paper is actually raised to where you can feel the seal. With that seal comes all the authority of the state. The seal allows the holder of that document to exercise all the authority given to them by the court in that document. It can award monetary gain or take it away. It can grant someone their freedom or take it away. It can take a life or spare it.

Jesus was acknowledged by the Father at His baptism when the Spirit of God came on Him and spoke: "This is my Son, whom I love; with him I am well pleased" (Matthew 3:16–17 NIV). "The Father loves the Son and has placed *everything* in his hands" (John 3:35 NIV, emphasis mine). With the death of Christ, He signed His name over ours to take our sin and death sentence: "She will give birth to a son, and you are to give him the name Jesus, because he will save his people from their sins" (Matthew 1:21 NIV). With His resurrection, we have new life, and with His ascension to heaven all authority is given to Him.

> I pray also that the eyes of your heart may be enlightened in order that you may know the hope to which he has called you, the riches of his glorious

inheritance in the saints, and his incomparably great power for us who believe. That power is like the working of his mighty strength, *which he exerted in Christ when he raised him from the dead and seated him at his right hand in the heavenly realms, far above all rule and authority, power and dominion, and every title that can be given, not only in the present age but also in the one to come. And God placed all things under his feet and appointed him to be head over everything for the church,*
Ephesians 1:18–22 NIV (emphasis mine)

When we repent and accept Him, Christ then seals us with His Spirit: "We know that we live in him and he in us, because he has given us of his Spirit" (1 John 4:13 NIV). And with that seal, everything that is Christ's is ours (Romans 8:15–17).

More Scriptures: John 10:28–29; 14:16–20; 17:1–4; 2 Corinthians 1:21–22

Take Action: *Be signed, sealed, and delivered through Jesus Christ our Lord.*

Prayer Requests/Answers:
_____
_____
_____
_____

You've Got a Friend in Him

> If you love me, show it by doing what I've told you. I will talk to the Father, and he'll provide you another Friend so that you will always have someone with you. This Friend is the Spirit of Truth. The godless world can't take him in because it doesn't have eyes to see him, doesn't know what to look for. But you know him already because he has been staying with you, and will even be *in* you!
>
> —John 14:15–17 MSG

I believe the Holy Spirit is probably the most misunderstood, underestimated, unappreciated, and untapped member of the Trinity. Maybe you have had a better grasp of Him and I'm just catching up. Sorry, slow learner.

Maybe the thought of Him in us scares us. Maybe it's the name: Holy Spirit or Holy Ghost. It conjures up an idea of some mystical figure appearing here and there, attempting to connect with us. But in John 14:16, the Holy Ghost is defined in different Bible versions as Comforter, Helper, Advocate, and Friend. Each description is essentially the same yet describing various responses of what He might be for us at significant times in our lives.

Jesus actually used the word *another* in that verse. For three years He had been all those things to His disciples and more. Maybe Jesus used that word to assure them they could trust the one Jesus was sending after Him. That having this Comforter, this Friend was like having Jesus back with them all the time. Maybe Jesus used that word for those of us who never saw Him face-to-face, never witnessed His miracles, and never experienced firsthand His crucifixion, His burial, or His resurrection. And because of that, we will have to believe although we cannot see, and hope although we cannot touch (Hebrews 11:1), and that the power in this other Friend is the same great power that was in Him and will give us the ability to do just that!

Maybe He wanted to assure us this Holy Ghost was much more than a mystical being but the third person of the Trinity, with whom we would share intimately. He would not only understand our pain but share with us in our sorrows, rejoice with us in our triumphs, guide us through the rough spots, and even endure the ordinary with us. He's never too bored with us; He's never too busy to be there for us. He is our comfort when no one or nothing else helps. He is there to guide us, correct us, and help us. He truly is our Friend.

> A friend loves at all times,
> —Proverbs 17:17 NIV

More Scriptures: John 15:26; 16:7–15; Romans 8:26; 1 Corinthians 2:10–14; 1 John 2:27

Take Action: *Earthly friends come and go; however, the Holy Spirit made plans not only to spend the here and now with you, but He will also be with us in eternity. Invite Him in to be your friend!*

Prayer Requests/Answers:
_____
_____
_____
_____

Teacher

> But the Comforter, *which is* the Holy Ghost, whom the Father will send in my name, he shall teach you all things, and bring all things to your remembrance, whatsoever I have said unto you.
> —John 14:26 KJV

The more I learn of God, the more amazed and humbled I become. I use the word *humble* because I am continually in awe of how our Creator cares for me as much as I have found He does, and that it is for no other reason than He chooses to. I am learning that nothing separates us from God's love, even our own stupidity (Romans 8:38–39).

I am learning I am a spectacular, unique creation, and the plans God has in store for me far exceed my own imagination! And thank God for that. As I see some unfold from time to time, I am simply blown away (Jeremiah 29:11).

I am learning that His forgiveness is complete and constant (Psalm 103:12), but I must ask for it. It is always my choice (1 John 1:9–10). I am also learning that because He has forgiven me for so much, through Him I *can* forgive others for much (Matthew 5:7; Philippians 4:13).

I am learning I need to trust His leading in my life, for He alone has the best in mind for me. When I allow others to influence my decisions or when I go off on my own (which is usually the case), the peace and joy disappear (Psalm 1:1–3; Proverbs 3:5–7). Eventually I see the error of my ways, and still I find there is no condemnation but open arms and never an "I told you so" attitude. It is one full of love, forgiveness, and acceptance through Christ and an "Okay, let's start again" (Psalm 32:5).

I am learning He is *always* fighting on my behalf for the battle is the Lord's (1 Samuel 17:47). There are many things I do not see with these human eyes, and sometimes it might be a good thing I can't (Isaiah 41:10; Zechariah 4:6; Ephesians 6:11–12).

I am learning that He is with me even during those times when life is unfair and I don't feel His presence. I realize my doubt comes in when I have taken my eyes off the Good Shepherd (Psalm 23) and put them on myself or the circumstance again (Isaiah 40:31; Romans 8:28).

I am learning to listen for God in the ordinary and let Him rule there as well, because it takes allowing the divine to live there, as much as it does to live in the crisis situations (Philippians 4:11–12; 1 Timothy 6:6–7).

I have found He is an exceptional teacher. I, however, at times am a lousy student … but I am learning!

> But as it is written, Eye hath not seen, nor ear heard, neither have entered into the heart of man, the things which God hath prepared for them that love him. But God hath revealed *them* unto us by his Spirit: for the Spirit searcheth all things, yea, the deep things of God.
>
> 1 Corinthians 2:9–10 KJV

More Scriptures: 1 Samuel 16:7; Isaiah 64:4; Jeremiah 31:3; 33:3

Take Action: *You will never be taught by a better teacher than the Holy Spirit. Come join the class with me.*

A Glimpse of God

Prayer Requests/Answers:
_____
_____
_____
_____

Equipment Man

> And behold, I am sending forth the promise of My Father upon you; but you are to stay in the city until you are clothed with power from on high.
> —Luke 24:49 NASB

Wow, clothed with power from on high! I wonder what the disciples were thinking when Jesus made that statement. If I had been there, I probably would have been thinking that maybe He means the power He had to perform all those miracles. That would be kind of cool. They came to find out that is exactly what they got, and much more. It literally transforms us into children of God.

"Not by might, nor by power, but by my spirit, saith the LORD of hosts" (Zechariah 4:6 KJV). The Holy Spirit gives you faith to believe God is working in you and the faithfulness to hang on while He does. This can only come through a continual surrender of our will. For He is a gentleman and He will not make us surrender ourselves to Him. It must be our choice. I know all too well how difficult it is sometimes to surrender myself to Him in my own life. God tells us what we need to do, but knowing we can't do it on our own; He gives us the "equipment" so we can—the Holy Spirit!

He's our equipment man. He fits each piece to meet our precise need. We are in a battle for our time and resources, our wants and desires, most surely our very lives. We must allow Him to equip us and not try to do it on our own.

> A final word: Be strong in the Lord and in his mighty power. Put on all of God's armor so that you will be able to stand firm against all strategies of the devil. For we are not fighting against flesh-and-blood

A Glimpse of God

> enemies, but against evil rulers and authorities of the unseen world, against mighty powers in this dark world, and against evil spirits in the heavenly places. Therefore, put on every piece of God's armor so you will be able to resist the enemy in the time of evil. Then after the battle you will still be standing firm. Stand your ground, putting on the belt of truth and the body armor of God's righteousness. For shoes, put on the peace that comes from the Good News so that you will be fully prepared. In addition to all of these, hold up the shield of faith to stop the fiery arrows of the devil. Put on salvation as your helmet, and take the sword of the Spirit, which is the word of God.
>
> —Ephesians 6:10–17 NLT

However, the process is not just to transform us, not just to protect us, but to perfect us into the image of Christ (Ephesians 4:11–13). As Paul wrote, even if our lives contained all the power that Christ displayed during His time on earth, but did not have the one element that set Christ apart from all others—His great love for all mankind—we are nothing. As our equipment man, His equipment is the best for He gives of Himself. As we are being perfected, others see the love and power of Christ displayed in our lives. And maybe because of our example, someone will choose to let Christ transform them as well into a child of God. You know what *real power* looks like: "But the fruit of the Spirit is love, joy, peace, patience, kindness, goodness, faithfulness, gentleness, self-control; against such things there is no law" (Galatians 5:22–23 NASB). The evidence of the Spirit within us is displaying His fruit in our lives, the greatest of these being love for each other.

More Scriptures: 1 Corinthians 2:5; 2 Corinthians 13:4; Ephesians 3:16–19; Philippians 1:6

Debra Niswander

Take Action: *Join the team and get equipped for the adventure of your life! The results—Christ perfected in us—are better than a championship ring or trophy, a gold medal, a green jacket, or even a Stanley Cup.*

Prayer Requests/Answers:
_____
_____
_____
_____

Road Maps and GPS

> All scripture is given by inspiration of God, and is profitable for doctrine, for reproof, for correction, for instruction in righteousness:
> —2 Timothy 3:16 KJV

> But when He, the Spirit of truth, comes, He will guide you into all the truth; for He will not speak on His own initiative, but whatever He hears, He will speak; and He will disclose to you what is to come.
> —John 16:13 NASB

With all the technology today there are many people who use a GPS system when they travel. I guess you could call it a "map with a voice." I actually love printed maps. I like to have them with me, especially when I travel long distances. I usually look at my whole course, plotting which roads I'm going to take, even if I've been that way many times before. I glance at the map often. Something about seeing where I started, where I'm at along the way, and where I'm supposed to end up is reassuring. I also watch the road signs along the way for problems or detours. Usually, I'm a pretty good navigator.

However, I have gotten turned around when I got off at an exit looking for something. Maybe I was using the GPS but wasn't listening to "Ethel" (one of my names for the GPS) very well. Because you know she can be annoying when she repeatedly tries to correct you. Or maybe I missed an exit because of a distraction or I decided to change the route on my own. I've ended up going out of my way or gotten lost. So I have to stop and double-check the map or "Ethel" to figure a way to get back on course.

Debra Niswander

I've heard it said the Bible is the great road map for life. It's God's written directions. So I guess you could say the Holy Spirit would be the GPS system, or God's "map with a voice." (And no, I don't call Him "Ethel.") I like to have both the Bible and the Holy Spirit with me wherever I go. Although I've read many verses over and over, I still read them to make sure I stay on the right road. I know where I started (in sin), and because of Christ where I am now (righteous in His sight), and I can see where I'm seeking to end (in heaven). I try to listen to the voice of the Holy Spirit to keep me on the right roads and heading in the right direction.

Sometimes though, it's hard to stay on that course plotted by God (Jeremiah 29:11). Even when I am following the Bible and trying to listen to the Spirit, I become distracted or don't heed the warning signs along the way (and yes, I get annoyed at the Spirit's correction because I know I should listen but I don't want to) or maybe I just decide to go another way on my own. And so I get turned around or even a little lost.

The wonderful thing about God is that He always provides a way to get back on course (1 John 1:9; 2:1). His Spirit leads me back to the Word (Hebrews 12:5–11). There isn't a path we've taken that God can't re-plot for us. With the wrong turns we make, the detours we take, even when we've gotten ourselves lost, He doesn't leave us stranded. He places signs along the way and His Spirit speaks to us to get our attention. So we have to stop and double-check that map (Bible) and listen to that GPS (Holy Spirit) to get us back on course.

> The entrance of your words gives light; it gives understanding to the simple.
> —Psalm 119:130 NIV

More Scriptures: Psalm 73:24; 111:10; 119:10, 12, 33, 81; Proverbs 3:5–6; 21:21; John 8:12; 10:17

A Glimpse of God

Take Action: *So don't forget to always have that map open and that GPS on, and God will always steer you in the right direction. We just have to be smart enough to actually listen.*

Prayer Requests/Answers:
_____
_____
_____
_____

Don't Turn Off the Faucet

> Now on the last day, the great *day* of the feast, Jesus stood and cried out, saying, "If anyone is thirsty, let him come to Me and drink. He who believes in Me, as the Scripture said, 'From his innermost being will *flow* rivers of living water.'" But this He spoke of the Spirit, whom those who believed in Him were to receive; for the Spirit was not yet *given*, because Jesus was not yet glorified.
> —John 7:37–39 NASB (emphasis mine)

I came to really appreciate the concept of "living water" on my recent mission trips to Africa. I went over with some friends of Fruit of the Vine Ministries as an outreach to help Pastor Moses Omondi Odhiambo whom they had met several years earlier. He started a ministry in his home village and we were there to help in whatever way we could. Until a few years ago, the only water they had access to, unless they could possibly afford to buy it, was catching rainwater or using the river/creek that runs through their village and farms. They wash their clothes in it, bathe in it, and their animals use it, and so you can see the cause for concern. Pastor Moses' ministry raised funds to dig a well for the village that his father oversees. The new well, I believe, goes down close to four hundred feet where the water is clean and pure. I thought about how I take for granted that I can walk into my kitchen anytime, turn on my faucet, and out flows clean, fresh water.

And I thought as well what a wonderful analogy of what Jesus does when we accept Him and the Holy Spirit comes to dwell in us. Yes, I've heard the analogy before, but maybe it really struck me this time because of what I was experiencing. From the depths of that well comes living water for those villagers. And as Jesus told us, with

A Glimpse of God

the indwelling of the Holy Spirit, out of our innermost being flows living water. The water from the well feeds our bodies, the water from Jesus feeds our spirits (Psalm 63:1; Isaiah 12:3; John 4:14; 6:35; Revelation 22:1).

But what really struck me was the word *flow*. As I searched the Bible, I found Scripture after Scripture of how God's Spirit would be *poured* out on us with *power* and would *flow* (Proverbs 1:23; Joel 2:28–29; Luke 24:49; Ephesians 6:10). My dad and I were discussing the flow of the Spirit and why sometimes it seems nominal in our lives. His comment was something like, "Well, we have the control valve." A light went off in my head when he said that. I thought about the faucet in my kitchen. The more water I want, the farther I turn the handle. If I only open it a little, I only get a trickle; if I open it wide, the water comes out full blast.

So the Spirit is inside us and we have the handle; it's our will. If we want the Spirit to flow a little, we'll only open our will to His leading a little. If we want the Spirit to be completely gushing out of us, we'll open our will to His leading in everything. I wonder how often we turn the handle of our will down or even off and then can't understand why we seem so dry and parched. Yeah, that's what I was thinking as well ... all too often. "Do *not* put out the Spirit's fire;" (1 Thessalonians 5:19 NIV, emphasis mine).

> I pray that out of his glorious, unlimited resources he will empower you with inner strength through his Spirit. ... Now all glory to God, through his mighty power at work within us, to accomplish infinitely more than we might ask or think.
> —Ephesians 3:16, 20 NASB

More Scriptures: Isaiah 32:15; 44:3; Zechariah 4:6; Romans 5:5

Take Action: So ... *let's open that faucet all the way and let His Spirit pour out of us. The cool thing is we won't get a water bill! God gives it freely.*

Prayer Requests/Answers:
_____
_____
_____
_____

You're Not Alone
(Our Swimming Instructor—Our Strength)

> that He would grant you, according to the riches of His glory, to be strengthened with might through His Spirit in the inner man,
>
> —Ephesians 3:16 NKJV

Loss takes many forms: a friendship, a love, the life of a loved one, an idea, a dream. A friend and I were talking about those losses, about working through them and at times how hard and how long it takes us. We all want to avoid those difficult situations that put the loss in front of us.

Sometimes you have to step away mentally to work through a problem. It doesn't mean you're ignoring the loss or the people who want to support you. Many times you feel alone even though you have all these people around you, because your mind is going a million miles a minute trying to deal with life in general as well as the loss itself. And you don't know what to do or how to handle it all. Sometimes you don't even know how to pray. Sometimes you just need to take a breath.

I think healing and working through loss comes in stages, in steps. What one person can work through in a short time might take someone else much longer. But peace can come with each step you take in the process. If you feel you're alone, don't believe it. The Holy Spirit is there to be your strength. And He knows how to pray to the Father even when you don't, even when you can't express it in words (Romans 8:26–27).

It's like if you're afraid of the water, you don't immediately jump in over your head to conquer your fear. Sometimes you have to stand at the shore for a while and just put your feet in. Then you go in to your knees and stand for a while. Then after a little bit longer, you move out to where the water is at your waist. Maybe the waist is as far as you'll ever be able to get, because it's not actually how far you went into the water that matters, it's the fact you got in the water at all.

You have to try to at least be willing to stand at the shore to begin the process. The fact of the matter is that the Holy Spirit is on the shore and He takes each step with you into the water. He's like having a swimming instructor standing there before you go into the water. Just knowing He's there gives you the strength to even try: "Finally, my brethren, be strong in the Lord, and in *the power of His might*" (Ephesians 6:10 NKJV, emphasis mine). It's not really your strength you're leaning on, but the fact that you know the swimming instructor is the expert and is right there with you. His strength becomes your strength to make each new move toward healing, toward growing, toward learning—toward whatever the Lord has in store. "I can do all things through Christ who strengthens me" (Philippians 4:13 NASB).

> He gives strength to the weary, And to *him who* lacks might He increases power.
> —Isaiah 40:29 NASB

More Scriptures: 2 Samuel 22:3; 1 Chronicles 16:11; Job 4:4; Psalm 118:14; 119:28; 121:1–2; 138:3; 147:5; 2 Corinthians 12:9; Ephesians 1:17–19

Take Action: *Begin your journey by stepping onto the shore. The Holy Spirit will be your instructor and guide. Trust in Him to be the strength you need no matter how deep you go.*

A Glimpse of God

Prayer Requests/Answers:
_____
_____
_____
_____

Our Conqueror

> For our struggle is not against flesh and blood, but against the rulers, against the authorities, against the powers of this dark world and against the spiritual forces of evil in the heavenly realms.
> —Ephesians 6:12 NIV

We can't get around the fact that in our heart of hearts we know that there's more to life than what we see with our natural eyes. Movies, TV shows, and books all reflect our fascination that there is this tremendous fight between good and evil and that the human race is smack dab in the middle of it—and that it will eventually come to a showdown with eternal consequences.

So many of the movies or TV shows like to interject one human being or a group of humans who take on the forces of evil or even nature, whatever that may look like—a meteor racing toward earth, Satan's spawn bent on devouring everything in their path, etc.—and just at the last second, this person or group of people save all of mankind. Maybe it's our need to believe *we* have the power to save ourselves.

We got it half right. It is a human being who saves the world, just not in the fashion we imagined. Because a human disobeyed his Creator and brought evil and sin into man's nature, a human had to conquer evil and sin to restore man's nature and man's relationship with his Creator (Romans 5:18–19). Since we are not just flesh and blood, but a soul and spirit as well, and because we must remain in our bodies for now, the battle rages on (Galatians 5:16–17). It will come to a showdown that no movie or TV show can rival. But here's the good news: I've read the end of the real book and *good* wins!

A Glimpse of God

You might say, okay, if your God is the real God, why all this? Well, although I believe we will never quite understand or see the full picture this side of heaven, I believe it boils down to choice. Satan chose to disobey; God chose to kick him out of eternity. We chose to disobey; God chose to redeem us. We were both created by God. Satan knew the riches of heaven yet he wanted to exalt himself. We want the riches of heaven and believe we can get there on our own, not realizing the riches of heaven is God Himself.

So, let's go back to the struggle and the battle that rages on. Life was not supposed to be the way it is. Man chose the direction of human life by rejecting God in the garden and believing Satan's version of life. But God, knowing all things, knew we would need a Savior. Our hero, Jesus, came just at the right moment, brandishing His weapon, the cross. He then walked off into the sunset, leaving a power (the Holy Spirit) for our use that strikes terror in the forces of evil. For through His Spirit and in His name, all the weapons formed against us are crushed. His Spirit is the conqueror (Romans 8:37) we use against the evil forces battling against us. Take that, you evil forces!

> The weapons we fight with are not the weapons of this world. On the contrary, they have divine power to demolish strongholds.
> —2 Corinthians 10:4 NIV

More Scriptures: Isaiah 54:17; Jeremiah 51:20; Zechariah 4:6

Take Action: *Your conqueror, the Holy Spirit, will fight for you relentlessly. Let Him!*

Debra Niswander

Prayer Requests/Answers:
_____
_____
_____
_____

Our Producer

> But the Spirit produces the fruit of love, joy, peace, patience, kindness, goodness, faithfulness, gentleness, self-control. There is no law that says these things are wrong.
> —Galatians 5:22–23 NCV

Have you ever looked at your life as a film still in the production stage? If so, who's producing it? Is it the circumstances you face, is it you, is it someone else? Who is developing your character?

Just like a film producer oversees and brings to completion a film project, so the Holy Spirit works in us to perfect us into the image of Christ, if we let Him: "to be made new in the attitude of your minds; and to put on the new self, created to be like God in true righteousness and holiness" (Ephesians 4:23–24 NIV). Now we could try to independently produce our own film, as we so often do. But ultimately it will turn out to be some half-rate production with a mediocre portrayal of what God wants us to be.

See, at the end of this blockbuster called life, it won't matter how much money we made, how many things we have, or even how smart we become. What will matter is *who* we have become. Have we remained the same people? When others met us did they still see Debbie, or Mike, or Kelly, or John, or did they see Christ in us? "For we are His workmanship, created in Christ Jesus for good works, which God prepared beforehand so that we would walk in them" (Ephesians 2:10 NASB).

John the Baptist put it this way: "He must increase, but I must decrease" (John 3:30 KJV). Are we able, or even willing to surrender the development of our character to the producer, the Holy Spirit?

"I have been crucified with Christ and I no longer live, but Christ lives in me. The life I live in the body, I live by faith in the Son of God, who loved me and gave himself for me" (Galatians 2:20 NIV).

It's like we're the supporting actresses and actors. We let Christ show through us by the Spirit and God gets the glory. He is and should be the main character.

More Scriptures: Romans 6:4; 12:2; 13:14; 1 Corinthians 15:49; Philippians 1:6; Titus 3:5; 2 Peter 1:4

Take Action: *Let the Spirit produce your film, and the award that awaits you will be far better than any human accolades. "His lord said to him, 'Well done, good and faithful servant; you have been faithful over a few things, I will make you ruler over many things. Enter into the joy of your Lord'" (Matthew 25:23 NKJV).*

Prayer Requests/Answers:
_____
_____
_____
_____

But the Holy Spirit produces this kind of fruit in our lives: love, joy, peace, patience, kindness, goodness, faithfulness, gentleness, and self-control. There is no law against these things!

—Galatians 5:22–23 NLT

Part 4

The Fruit of the Spirit

The Fruit of the Spirit

> But the Holy Spirit produces this kind of fruit in our lives: joy, peace, patience, kindness, goodness, faithfulness, gentleness, and self-control. There is no law against these things.
> —Galatians 5:22–23 NLT

I don't know a lot about gardening but I do know that fruit can only be produced by the planting of the seed. The condition of the soil is paramount to the quality and bounty of the fruit. As human beings, we can display in some form these traits of the fruit mentioned above, but they will be flawed when produced under our own power because our soil is damaged.

When we accept Christ as Savior, God the Father sees Christ when He looks at us. God sees what Christ did for us in washing away our sin. He makes each of us a new creature in this process and our hearts (our spirits) now become good and fertile soil: "A good man out of the good treasure of the heart bringeth forth good things; and an evil man out of the evil treasure bringeth forth evil things." (Matthew 12:35 KJV).

The "seeds" of His fruit are planted in our hearts. The Spirit, as we allow Him, nurtures and waters those seeds. Because we know that He has to "prune" us (John 15:2), as we grow and mature in Him through that pruning, we begin to live a life that bears fruit of love, joy, peace, and so on. When our fruit comes from the "seeds" of *His* Spirit, and not from ourselves, we bear the likeness of those seeds: Christ. Christian character is produced by the Holy Spirit, not by our self-effort. And this life, reflecting Christ, is what is pleasing to the Father (John 15:1–5; Galatians 2:20).

Spirit-produced fruit bears *love* that is pure and perfect—God's agape love. *Joy* and *peace*—centering on the acute awareness of where you were without Christ and where you are now. *Patience*, or a "waiting on the Lord"—honed from practicing the art of surrender. *Kindness*—replacing the need to "get" with the desire to "give." *Goodness*—the outward appearance of the inward dwelling of God, the only one who *is* truly good. *Faith*—believing when there is no physical reason to believe, because your belief is based on the integrity of God (Hebrews 11:1). *Gentleness/meekness*—sensitivity to others; understanding that it is by God's grace you stand redeemed and therefore cannot claim you did it yourself (Ephesians 2:8–9). *Self-control*—because of *His* Spirit in you and Him renewing your spirit, you desire to reflect the appearance of Jesus rather than yourself.

LOVE

A Perfect Love

> There is no fear in love. But perfect love drives out fear, because fear has to do with punishment. The man who fears is not made perfect in love.
> —1 John 4:18 NIV

I'm sure most would say there is no perfect love. Even in a good relationship, whether it's between parent and child, husband and wife, or friends, there are disagreements, arguments, selfishness, and quite often hurt feelings. Some relationships are never repaired. So, it is true that the "love" we have and show is not perfect. It comes from us, and since we are not perfect, how can our love be perfect?

However, there is one perfect love, and I have experienced it. God's love for each of us is a perfect love (agape love—John 3:16). His love covers all our sins, failures, and selfishness, and it takes our fear away. His love makes us lovable and able to love. He can't stop thinking about us (Psalm 139:17–18). When He looks at us He smiles.

God's love is unconditional. It is never withheld from us, even when we sin against Him. Nothing separates us from that love (Romans 8:38–39), even when we are at our worst. He won't force His love. In fact, He loves us enough to let us choose to love Him, and He still loves us even when we don't love Him back. When God sees us, He looks past the worst in us and sees what we are in Christ or what we can be if we choose Him. God allowed the one He loved the most, Jesus, to take our place, because that is how much He loves us.

What's the catch? That's just it, there isn't one. We just have to accept His love. Once we truly do, we want to love Him back. Once we do, we want to love others with that kind of love. Once we have been touched by that love, we can love others as God does. We can see others as God sees them, for when He sees *each of us*, He sees Christ in us. We can love with the love we have received from Him, that perfect love.

It's so simple that it's hard, because although we want to be loved like that, it frightens us. Maybe we've been hurt by love, and we are afraid to be hurt again. Maybe we feel we have to prove ourselves to have this love. But we don't. This love is not like any other love we've experienced. Maybe we're afraid we can't return love like that (because honestly we're selfish). We can't on our own. We can do this only when we accept and allow *His perfect love* to live in us: "And now these three remain: faith, hope and love. But the greatest of these is love" (1 Corinthians 13:13 NIV).

> We love him, because he first loved us.
> —1 John 4:19 KJV

More Scriptures: Romans 5:8; 1 John 3:23–24

Take Action: *Of all the things we could strive to be perfect at, wouldn't love be the best one? Through Him we can.*

Prayer Requests/Answers:
_____
_____
_____
_____

Choices

> This is how God showed his love among us: He sent his one and only Son into the world that we might live through him. This is love: not that we loved God, but that he loved us and sent his Son as an atoning sacrifice for our sins.
>
> 1 John 4:9–10 NIV

> We love because he first loved us.
>
> 1 John 4:19 NIV

What causes us to make the choices we make? Sometimes they are not for the best of reasons. And then, sometimes the choices we make aren't based on our desires, but on the love we have for someone else. Sometimes because of love, we choose to sacrifice even our own desires to put the needs and wants of the ones we love first.

"Because I love you, I have to choose to accept your decision. It doesn't mean you have lost my love. I simply choose to love you even knowing you might not love me back."

After penning those words, I heard the sweet voice of God say, *Now you know how I feel. Because I love you, I let you make the choice to love Me back. And just so you know, My love for you does not depend on your love for Me. I'll never take it back. I am always here waiting, loving you just the same.* "But God shows his great love for us in this way: Christ died for us while we were *still* sinners" (Romans 5:8 NCV, emphasis mine).

I don't think we really can comprehend that kind of love, that kind of sacrifice, that kind of choice. I realized how shallow and incomplete my love can be compared to God's love. How often I put conditions or restrictions on my love. How selfish my love can be. I don't really want my love to be that way, but it certainly can be.

After hearing those words from God, I was ashamed, but at the same time I felt something amazing. There was no hint of anger or condemnation in what God said, just the assurance that His love was there no matter what. His love, so deep and complete, reached across time and chose a place in history to demonstrate that love through Jesus (Ephesians 1:4–5). *All* I have to do is choose. It always comes down to choice. *So, I am choosing to get out of the way and receive God and His love in my life, because I want to love like He does, deep and complete without conditions and restrictions.* Some days the choice is easy and then some days it's not so easy. *But* I'm still choosing.

More Scriptures: John 13:34; 1 John 4:7–21

Take Action: *It is easy to love those who love you back. The true test of God's love in you is to choose to love the ones who don't.*

Prayer Requests/Answers:

_____
_____
_____
_____

A Shared Love

(written February 2009)

> Love is patient, love is kind *and* is not jealous; love does not brag *and* is not arrogant.
> —1 Corinthians 13:4 NASB

This was written for my son Jared and his wife, Ashley, for their wedding, February 14, 2009. Love shared through their relationship with Jesus Christ. Here is my paraphrase of 1 Corinthians 13:4–9:

How do I know I love you?

I know because I realize time schedules aren't always important, but any time with you is. Please understand me should I forget.

How do I know I love you?

I know because I want to give to you out of my whole heart. Please believe me should I fail.

How do I know I love you?

I know because I want to trust your love for me. Please love me still should I show fear and disrespect.

How do I know I love you?

I know because I am humbled that God has blessed my life with your presence. Please overlook my attitude when I forget that blessing.

How do I know I love you?

I know because I want to always show you my love through my words and actions. Please forgive me when I have caused you hurt instead.

How do I know I love you?

I know because my heart smiles when I think of you and always will. May my heart be allowed to have a lifetime of smiles with you.

> [Love] bears all things, believes all things, hopes all things, endures all things. Love never fails. ... And now these three remain: faith, hope and love. But the greatest of these is love.
> —1 Corinthians 13:7–8 NKJV;
> 1 Corinthians 13:13 NIV

More Scriptures: Proverbs 10:12; 1 Peter 4:8–9; 1 John 4:12

Take Action: *We can have a relationship like that if we first have one with Him. Don't wait any longer.*

Prayer Requests/Answers:

_____
_____
_____
_____

A Broken Heart Healed

> The Lord is close to the brokenhearted and saves those who are crushed in spirit.
> —Psalm 34:18 NIV

Have things so crushed you that your heart literally feels like it's broken? If you have, this verse is for you. This is difficult to put in print, but I know I have to. These devotionals are as much for me to heal and grow and change as for anyone else.

I made a decision several years ago to seek a divorce. It was the most excruciating decision I've ever made. I felt like I failed as a Christian, as a wife, and as a mother, but everything I tried and prayed for didn't seem to change the situation. I know many will say that divorce is never the answer for a Christian, but I also believe God will only work in someone's life by permission. Both partners need to surrender to God first, and I could not carry the load for both. Some hurts are so intense and they cause so much weariness that it literally crushes you. Even though we sometimes try to carry the load alone, we aren't mean to. Jesus tells us to lean on Him (1 Peter 5:6–7). I have realized since then, I was trying to carry all the load myself. I had taken my eyes off the Lord and put it on the situation and the person. In doing so I was engulfed and overwhelmed.

In saying all that, I accept my own faults. I face and fight them daily—stubbornness and opinionated, to name a few. I am sure my friends and family could add to the list. However, this is not about fault on either side, but about healing.

I know that by making this decision, I caused pain to my children, and I am so sorry for that. I live each day with that knowledge. It truly was not my intention to cause them or even my ex-husband any pain, but the hurt was so intense it had overwhelmed my entire being. Maybe you have been there. In everything I have experienced and am experiencing about God, I believe He understands our frailty, our breaking points, our need to withdraw. For all the pain we inflict on each other, His love is constant and His healing is as near as a whispered plea for help. But sometimes the hurt from others has become so loud we can't hear the *Lord* answering that plea. That was me. But God knows that and He waits.

So how did the healing come? It has been a process, and that process continues daily. I have tried to stop looking at the one who hurt me (whoever that might be) and look at the *One* who heals me. I am trying to finally listen wholeheartedly to the Lord. I'm confessing my own sins and *really allowing* God's grace to cover them all. I'm forgiving myself. I'm learning it is not my job to save others—God does that. But they have to choose to let God do that, and I *can't* make them and God *won't* make them. I'm surrendering my expectation and my idea of my life and just trying to walk by His direction and not my own. I'm learning to enjoy the peace in that. I'm wanting to really forgive others and *giving up* those hurts caused by them, because sometimes I wear them as a badge of honor to use as an excuse. I am replacing those hurts with *God Himself.* At the end of the day, I have His love, and that's good enough for me. And I'm especially trying to humbly ask forgiveness not only of the ones I hurt but also of the ones who hurt me.

> Answer me, O LORD, out of the goodness of your love; in your great mercy turn to me.
> —Psalm 69:16 NIV

More Scriptures: Psalm 61:1–3; 119:50; 147:3; Song of Solomon 2:4; 2 Corinthians 1:3–4; 2 Thessalonians 2:16–17

A Glimpse of God

Take Action: *Take the pieces of your heart out of the hands of those who hurt you, and put them into God's hands. Let Him put them back together.*

Prayer Requests/Answers:
_____
_____
_____
_____

JOY

Stuffed

> You will make known to me the path of life; in Your presence is fullness of joy; in Your right hand there are pleasures forever.
>
> —Psalm 16:11 NASB

Fullness of joy. I was trying to wrap my head around that particular phrase when I asked my dad for some help. My dad is great at giving in-depth answers. He gave me an illustration of the meaning of joy in this particular Scripture. Maybe he had heard it before or maybe it was his own, but I loved it. He described it as sitting down for a great meal and you have eaten so much that you are completely stuffed. You couldn't hold another bite, *but* the meal was so good you want more. That's the joy of God's presence.

That description so fit what happened to me the other day going to work. I even shared it with probably my whole e-mail list. I'm sure some of them thought I had lost it again, but I didn't mind. See, that morning I woke up in one of those moods where you just want to pull the covers over your head and declare a mental health day. It took some doing to drag myself out of bed. But I was so glad I did.

I live in northern Michigan where sometimes winter lasts the whole year except July 4 (just kidding, but some winters feel that long). So my drive back and forth to work can be an adventure. The one thing that saves me some days is the sunrises and sunsets. Often, I have literally pulled over on the edge of the road to witness the unfolding of a miracle. On this particular morning it was breathtaking. The streaks of yellow, orange, and pink rose from the horizon and catapulted across the sky.

As I wrote to my e-mail friends, you may say what you want—that it is the gases coming together, doing this and doing that to make the colors form—but ride in the car with me one day and you'll change your mind. God's presence fills my car, and sometimes I cry because it is so real. I feel like God is saying hello and inviting me to be in His presence, letting me know that I am in the palm of His hand and how much He loves me. I felt like I was having that meal my dad described. I was stuffed full, but I wanted more.

A couple of days later, I thought how it is easy to recognize and feel the presence of God on days like that. A view that spectacular raises your awareness. Today, however, I'm looking out the window, eating my lunch, and I see winter: cold, windy, a storm in the forecast. Then all of a sudden I sense God's presence and Him saying, *Excuse Me, I'm here now too.* I smiled and laughed out loud, because God's presence in this moment is as real and touching as the day of the beautiful sunrise and I am "full of joy" once again.

Real joy, lasting joy, fullness of joy. How can we have it? I'm thinking that being in God's presence is a good bet. And I'm thinking it can be anywhere or anytime. But it can go beyond that, because every spiritual fruit we display comes in having the presence of God within us by the salvation of Jesus Christ and the indwelling of His Spirit. It is to be as natural as it is to breathe. We can be stuffed, not just with joy, but with love, kindness, and on and on. And we can share that with others so they can be stuffed too!

> These things I have spoken to you so that My joy may
> be in you and *that* your joy might be full.
> —John 15:11 NASB

More Scriptures: Psalm 21:6; 34:4; 63:7; John 17:13; 1 John 1:4

A Glimpse of God

Take Action: *Be <u>stuffed</u> with God's presence. You'll want more and the great thing is that you'll never need to go on a diet.*

Prayer Requests/Answers:
_____
_____
_____
_____

Eternal Optimist

> Consider it pure joy, my brothers, whenever you face trials of many kinds, because you know that the testing of your faith develops perseverance. Perseverance must finish its work so that you may be mature and complete, not lacking anything.
>
> James 1:2–4 NIV

Are you a glass-half-empty or a glass-half-full kind of person? Typically I'm the half-full kind, but I must admit I've been known to vent or whine about rough circumstances that have fallen into my glass. Sometimes it is hard to swallow.

Circumstances—difficult ones especially—can certainly rob us of those joyful feelings. How can we "count it all joy" when we go through tough experiences? We are such emotional creatures. We react to situations based many times on the memories of how we felt in a past situation. Okay, I'll admit that at times I am controlled by my emotions and don't always handle myself well. (And those who know me are saying, "No, really!") But I think we were designed to have emotions. Just look at the fruits of the Spirit. There are emotions all over those fruit (Galatians 5:22–23). And it doesn't say "the fruit of Debbie." It has to do with who is in control of them—me or the Holy Spirit. When His Spirit controls our emotions, it's not that we don't have them; it's just that they are pure, they are appropriate, they glorify God.

But the other aspect of that Scripture is the reason for the testing. It's to make us strong, to endure until the end, because what is to come will blow us away. It will all be worth it. Jesus assured us that although things might be tough, there will still be victory: "These things I have spoken unto you, that in me ye might have peace. In the world ye shall have tribulation: but be of good cheer; I have overcome the world" (John 16:33 KJV). He was tempted by the same things, endured the same trials. It wasn't just the beating, the crown of thorns thrust onto His head, the nails in His feet and hands, but the shame of the cross. He was treated like a criminal. He took the guilt of every cruel behavior that man could ever conceive to do to another human being, but had never done them. Everything that is completely and utterly against God, Jesus took upon Himself and paid the price for us. He endured it for the *joy* of knowing that you and I would sit down with Him on His throne (Revelation 3:21). If that doesn't make you an optimist, nothing will. It makes me want to hang on till the end.

Talk about a perfect example of enduring something to the end: "Looking unto Jesus the author and the finisher of *our* faith; who for the joy that was set before him endured the cross, despising the shame, and is set down at the right hand of the throne of God" (Hebrews 12:2 KJV).

With that knowledge of eternity just the other side of this life and a seat reserved if we so choose, we can handle those things with joy, with grace, with love, with mercy, and with hope through His Spirit.

> Dear friends, do not be surprised at the painful trial you are suffering, as though something strange were happening to you. But rejoice that you participate in the sufferings of Christ, so that you may be overjoyed when his glory is revealed.
> —1 Peter 4:12–13 NIV

More Scriptures: Micah 7:8; Romans 8:37; 2 Corinthians 2:14; 4:7–18

Take Action: *Look beyond the problem; let the joy of your Lord be your strength.*

Prayer Requests/Answers:
_____
_____
_____
_____

Behind the Clouds

> Though the fig tree does not bud and there are no grapes on the vines, though the olive crop fails and the fields produce no food, though there are no sheep in the pen and no cattle in the stalls, yet I will rejoice in the LORD, I will be joyful in God my Savior.
> —Habakkuk 3:17–18 NIV

What is real joy? Is it a single, tangible feeling that radiates from within or a combination of moments or events we experience? Merrian-Webster.com indicates one definition as a "state of happiness or bliss," which means to me it is something constant and probably deep in us. But still, what would cause our joy to be able to be that constant, given the condition of the world these days or even our lives at times?

A friend of mine and I had been chatting and he made the statement, "I wish upon the stars." I thought it was a sweet statement. I did ask him though what he did when he couldn't see the stars, because you know they're still there even if you can't see them hidden by the clouds. Does he only wish upon a star if he can see it?

That brought me back to the thought of real joy. It seems to me that the ability to have a constant joy would have to be based on the confidence of what the joy is tied to or grounded in. Is the foundation solid? Can it be shaken if situations change around us? Can we still have it through tears, fears, and struggles? "These things have I spoken unto you, that my joy might remain in you, and *that* your joy might be full" (John 15:11 KJV). Prior to that statement, Jesus was telling us He is the True Vine and if we stay connected to Him we would truly flourish in a way uncommon to our natural selves. The first verse of the chapter before that says, "Let not your heart be troubled: ye believe in God, believe also in me" (KJV). Now doesn't that verse say it all?

So I stopped and thought again about wishing upon those stars. I know that if I could peel away the clouds, the stars would be there. I have confidence they don't leave when the clouds move in. And so I decided to peel away the clouds in my life; ideas of the world, the good, the bad, the troubles, the aches, the hurts, and the people. I found not just the stars, but the *One* who made them. I have joy because of Jesus Christ, my Savior, and the love He constantly shows me. He's deep and lasting. My confidence lies in Him and He doesn't leave even when the clouds move in. His love is amazing. And because my confidence is grounded in the Solid Rock, my foundation is sure. And so in those times when life tries to take my joy, I'll peel away those clouds again to see, as always, the Maker of the stars is still there! And I grab hold of that joy that needs no words.

> I delight greatly in the LORD; my soul rejoices in my God. For he has clothed me with garments of salvation and arrayed me in a robe of his righteousness, as a bridegroom adorns his head like a priest, and as a bride adorns herself with her jewels.
> —Isaiah 61:10 NIV

More Scriptures: Psalm 46:1–11; Proverbs 3:26; John 17:13; Romans 15:13; 2 Corinthians 5:5–7; Philippians 4:4; 1 Peter 1:6–9; 1 John 1:1–4

Take Action: *Come, peel away the clouds; the Maker of the stars is always there. Let your joy be in Him. It's solid!*

A Glimpse of God

Prayer Requests/Answers:
_____
_____
_____
_____

Who's Your Trustee?

> But let everyone who trusts you be happy; let them sing glad songs forever. Protect those who love you and who are happy because of you.
> —Psalm 5:11 NCV

> The LORD is my strength and shield. I trust him with all my heart. He helps me, and my heart is filled with joy. I burst out in songs of thanksgiving.
> —Psalm 28:7 NLT

In estate planning there is this procedure called a trust. You take all of what you value and own (monies, stocks, bonds, real estate, etc.) and place them in the trust for protection for your present and your future. You appoint a trustee to administer or follow the instructions and plans set forth in the trust. The trustee must be someone you believe will do what is always the best for you. If it is not yourself, you choose someone you are very secure with. In doing so, however, you realize the trustee cannot predict the future as to the ebb and flow of gains and losses on your assets, but it does bring a sense of peace and joy to know your assets are placed in some safety.

So can I propose to you that God made a trust for each of us in which we can place our valuables: our hopes, dreams, possessions, time, relationships, and our lives? We don't have to use the trust (that's why it's called free choice), but once we do, the best plan is to appoint Him as Trustee. By doing that we are saying we believe He will do what is best for us if we let Him follow the plans and instructions of the trust He prepared for us.

A Glimpse of God

> "For I know the plans I have for you," declares the LORD, "plans to prosper you and not to harm you, plans to give you hope and a future."
> —Jeremiah 29:11 NIV

> But as it is written: "Eye has not seen, nor ear heard, nor have entered into the heart of man the things which God has prepared for those who love Him.
> —1 Corinthians 2:9 NKJV

Joy and peace will come from feeling secure in who oversees our trust. We have confidence in the Trustee whom we have placed our lives in. We believe the Trustee will always do what is best for us even if the circumstances look tough and unclear. You see, God is one trustee who does not have to predict the future. He already knows the future, for *He* is the future. He knows what the ebb and flow of our lives will be, and He weathers each gain or loss with us: "And surely I will be with you always, to the very end of the age" (Matthew 28:20 NIV).

> Blessed *is* the man who makes the LORD his trust, and does not respect the proud, nor such as turn aside to lies.
> —Psalm 40:4 NKJV

More Scriptures: Psalm 9:10; 31:14; 33:21; 56:3–4; 62:8; Isaiah 26:3–4; Jeremiah 17:7

Take Action: *Set up your trust with God today. Experience the joy of being safe and secure with Him as your Trustee—now and into the future.*

Prayer Requests/Answers:
_____
_____
_____
_____

Living Trust

I gave this talk at our ladies' prayer breakfast (S.I.C.—Sisters in Christ) and had given them this attached living trust. They really liked it and thought I should include it in the book for anyone else who would like to have their own living trust. So I did.

Living Trust between God, Jehovah-jireh and _____

I, _____, hereby make God, Jehovah-jireh, also known as "My provider" the Trustee of this living trust, which would include my life. "Blessed is that man who makes the LORD his trust" (Psalm 40:4 NKJV).

By signing this trust, I hereby declare: "LORD, I trust you. I have said, 'You are my God.' My life is in your hands" (Psalm 31:14–15 NCV).

I agree to place into this trust, including but not limited to the following:

   A. My fears—"When I am afraid, I will trust you. I praise God for his word. I trust God, so I am not afraid. What can human beings do to me?" (Psalm 56:3–4 NCV).

   B. My problems—"People, trust God all the time. Tell him all your problems, because God is our protection" (Psalm 62:8 NCV).

   C. My time—"My times *are* in thy hand" (Psalm 31:15 KJV); "To every *thing there* is a season and a time to every purpose under heaven" (Ecclesiastes 3:1 KJV).

D. My dreams/my plans—"'For I know the plans I have for you,' declares the LORD, 'plans to prosper you and not to harm you, plans to give you hope and a future'" (Jeremiah 29:11 NIV); "But as it is written: 'Eye has not seen, nor ear heard, nor have entered into the heart of man the things which God has prepared for those who love Him.' But God has revealed *them* to us through His Spirit. For the Spirit searches all things, yes, the deep things of God" (1 Corinthians 2:9–10 NKJV).

E. My possessions—"Don't store treasures for yourselves here on earth where moths and rust will destroy them and thieves can break in and steal them. But store your treasures in heaven where they cannot be destroyed by moths or rust and where thieves cannot break in and steal them" (Matthew 6:19–20 NCV).

F. My relationships—"Do nothing out of selfish ambition or vain conceit, but in humility consider others better than yourselves. Each of you should look not only to your own interests, but also to the interests of others" (Philippians 2:3–4 NIV).

G. My life—"I was put to death on the cross with Christ, and I do not live anymore—it is Christ who lives in me. I still live in my body, but I live by faith in the Son of God who loved me and gave himself to save me" (Galatians 2:20 NCV).

For, "You, LORD, give true peace to those who depend on you, because they trust you. So, trust the LORD always, because he is our Rock forever" (Isaiah 26:3–4 NCV).

Signed hereto on this _____ day of the month of ____, in year _____ of our Precious Lord and Savior, Jesus Christ.

PEACE

He Holds On to You Even When You Can't or Won't Hold On to Him

> When you pass through the waters, I will be with you; and when you pass through the rivers, they will not sweep over you. When you walk through the fire, you will not be burned; the flames will not set you ablaze.
>
> —Isaiah 43:2 NIV

I must admit there was a time I wondered if God had fallen asleep on me. I was hit with one too many things in my life that I never saw coming. I didn't see how these could be good things. You know the saying that things come in threes? Well, I felt like I had surpassed that three mark. I was thinking if it didn't stop soon, I would have nothing.

I cried a lot, thought a lot, and I did pray (and ask why) a lot. This was one of those times where my expectation of what I thought my life was going to be met reality. I felt defeated and like a failure.

Then a question came to my mind: *Why do you feel defeated?* And my answer was, "Look at what's going on. My life has fallen apart." Then another question came: *By whose standards are you measuring your life—the world's or Mine?* God has a way of asking those tough questions and making me look at myself especially when I don't want to.

I thank the Lord for the many great pastors I have studied under over the years, because they all emphasized reading the Bible and memorizing God's words. Because, as they all said, when we struggle with life, not *if there is struggle*, but *when,* God will bring those words back to us when we need them. This was one of those times. Before I really had time to think about that measuring stick

I was using on my life, this Scripture came to mind: "God causes all things to work together for good to those who love God" (Romans 8:28 NASB).

And I knew the "all" even included the messes in my life that I have made myself and those I haven't. *If I let God*, He can use anything to bring me closer to Him. That is the goal God has for us in this journey of life—to know Him intimately and in that intimacy become like Him and follow His plan for our lives in preparing us for eternity with Him. "For I know the plans I have for you, declares the LORD, plans to prosper you and not to harm you, plans to give you hope and a future" (Jeremiah 29:11 NIV).

So I had to admit that I have taken the reins from God and headed off in my own direction at times (okay, *lots* of times). Then when problems came, I asked God what happened and where He was. Funny thing is He never left. And what I heard from Him brought the security I was looking for all along. His answer: *If you let Me, I'll work it out for good. Sit back, let Me drive from now on, and while I am, let Me give you this:* "I am leaving you with a gift—peace of mind and heart. And the peace I give is a gift the world cannot give. So don't be troubled or afraid" (John 14:27 NLT).

So now I know (and you, too) when those problems of our own doing and those that were not come into our lives, we can know God is holding on to us through it all. "I have told you these things, so that in *Me* you may have *peace*. In this world you will have trouble. *But take heart! I have overcome the world*" (John 16:33 NIV, emphasis mine).

More Scriptures: John 14:1; Philippians 4:7

Take Action: *Real peace is so hard to achieve on our own. The next time you feel the flames flicker or the waters rise, remember who is right there with*

A Glimpse of God

you and let Him give you His peace. And remember, God is fireproof and He walks on water.

Prayer Requests/Answers:
_____
_____
_____
_____

The Conquering "C"

(written in 2010)

> And the peace of God, which passeth all understanding, shall keep your hearts and minds through Christ Jesus.
> —Philippians 4:7 KJV

The "c" word. It strikes fear in anyone who hears it. It doesn't see color of skin, it doesn't distinguish between rich or poor, and it doesn't matter if you've led a good life or a not-so-good life. That word—*cancer*—takes one's breath away. Our hearts skip a beat at the mere mention of the word. I've heard it far too many times in the lives of family and friends than I care to think about. Many of them are no longer here.

But, with the anxiety and fear that this "c" word brings, there is another "C" word for handling it: Christ. Let me introduce you to two people who did that: one was my sister, and the other is my friend, Pam.

My sister, Jeannie, has been gone four years now. Some days it feels like it just happened and other days as if it is a dream and she is only a phone call away. We were like most sisters growing up. She was the older, bossy one and me, I was the annoying little sister (okay, and spoiled too). I think we overcame most of those childish issues, and over the years we became closer and closer. She loved being Aunt Jeannie to my boys.

Not very long after we had lost one uncle to cancer, another to a heart attack, and my brother to cancer, the news came. My heart felt like it literally broke when she first told me. I still can't imagine how she must have felt. Over the months, until her death, we talked and

A Glimpse of God

e-mailed a lot about everything and about nothing, just relishing in the ability to talk to each other. I am thankful for seeing her as well. As with most things like this, I only wished I had taken more opportunities to visit over the years. But I am thankful to have seen her before she died. (She lived in Virginia; I live in Michigan.)

The hardest thing for Jeannie was to leave her family, but her faith stayed strong. I'm not going to tell you she never wondered why. She was human—how could anyone not question? But she was so thankful for what Christ had done for her, including the many ways He had protected her during her "wild" years. She was not perfect, just forgiven. She kept her humor despite the pain she endured, and she always seemed to be smiling. Jeannie was the one comforting us at times when it should have been us comforting her.

I hope I can express this so you will understand. When she resigned herself to the fact that she was dying, it wasn't that she gave up. Jeannie wanted more than anything to live and she told me so, but she expressed that Christ had given her peace. She knew she wasn't alone. He was there with her, had always been there, and always would be. Her last breath here would be her first breath in eternity with Him.

She didn't concentrate on the "c" that had a hold of her physical body, but on the "C" that had a hold of her soul.

> For I am convinced that neither death nor life, neither angels nor demons, neither the present nor the future, nor any powers, neither height nor depth, nor anything else in all creation, will be able to separate us from the love of God that is in Christ Jesus our Lord.
> —Romans 8:38–39 NIV

More Scriptures: Isaiah 25:8; John 14:2; 1 Corinthians 15:54–57

Debra Niswander

Take Action: *Accept Christ's conquering peace over your life's struggles.*

Prayer Requests/Answers:
_____
_____
_____
_____

The Conquering "C" (continued)

(written in 2010)

Do not let your hearts be troubled. Trust in God; trust also in me.

—John 14:1 NIV

My friend, Pam, is currently going through treatment for cancer. I knew Pam and her family when I lived in Pittsburgh during my high school years. I remember so well her gentle spirit, kind heart, and sense of humor. There are people in your life that you have known over the years who come to mind when others speak about character, commitment, and faith. She is one of those. Like my sister, I am sure her e-mails bring more of a comfort to me than any of mine might bring to her.

I want to share with you the impact she has had on me. It has not been the details of her treatments, although, she keeps us updated on how they go and how she is feeling. These are the things you would expect her to include, and she certainly asks for prayer to get through the difficulty.

What amazes me is Pam's attitude and her other prayer requests. She is always asking us to pray for others she has met: other patients who are getting treatment, their families, and nurses and staff that she has met. She asks for the boldness to take opportunities to talk to them about her Christ that she loves so deeply. She credits the strength that she has to Him and Him alone. Her desire is to be a faithful witness of what Christ has done in her life. For her, this has been an opportunity to touch people's lives that she would never have come in contact with ordinarily. I am humbled. Usually, the e-mails are not long, but I am captivated when I read them, and I love the

Scripture verses she sends with them. They leave me exhilarated with a resolve to continue this walk of faith.

She doesn't concentrate on the "c" that has her physical body, but on the "C" that has her soul.

More Scriptures: Romans 5:1; Philippians 4:19; Colossians 3:15

Take Action: *Whatever your struggle is — anger, hurt, fear, sickness, whatever it may be—don't concentrate on that. Instead, concentrate on the "C"hrist who conquers them all.*

Prayer Requests/Answers:
_____
_____
_____
_____

Peace in Our Worries, in Our Fears, in the Unknown, in Our Hurts, in Our Prayers That Seem to Be No

> And we know that all things work together for good to them that love God, to them who are the called according to *his* purpose.
> —Romans 8:28 KJV

The pastor was recently preaching on Matthew 6:25–34, which deals with worry. It was a good sermon. It reminded me of a Bible course I took years ago. One particular night the teacher had us spend some time in prayer and journal what we believed God was impressing on our hearts, and then if we would consider sharing those thoughts with the class. Honestly, I don't remember the actual lesson, but I remember the journaling.

I probably only wrote one short paragraph. However, one statement in that paragraph stood out for me: *Worry is not a word I know.* The words were simple and powerful then, simple and powerful now. I really wish I had grasped what God was saying to me then. Why could I not see the bold, confident peace that exploded out of those seven words? Obviously He knew I would need it later, but why didn't I get it then? I can look back now on past situations, knowing if I had really let that truth sink in, although the situation might not have changed, my outlook on it might have. Maybe that's why He kept bringing it back over and over (told you I was a slow learner).

My God—who was, is, and shall be—does not concern Himself with worry. It never enters His heart. Why have I so long let it enter mine? Why have I not grasped who I am as a child of God?

It is not arrogance; it is humble confidence that the *One* who walked on the water, walks with me at each and every crossroad in my life.

You'll notice I didn't stop with just "worry" in the title of this devotional. How often we pray for God to take our worries, our fears, futures, hurts, and requests, but we only want the answers we want and when they don't come, the peace is not there and disappointment creeps in. Max Lucado has a great cure for disappointment: "Don't ask God to do what you want. Ask God to do what is right." That surely causes thoughts of repentance. If we believe God to be who He says He is, somehow we must work to believe the outcome will be the right outcome. We must engrave on our hearts and minds the verse above and each and every verse that says He loves us, He watches over us, and He fights for us despite what the outcome looks like (1 Peter 5:7). There truly is peace in that if we let it be ... and that peace defies all human understanding (Philippians 4:6–7). It's not really the lack of worry that's so amazing, but having the presence of the Prince of Peace in us that is.

> Do not be anxious about anything, but in everything, by prayer and petition, with thanksgiving, present your requests to God.
> —Philippians 4:6 NIV

More Scriptures: Psalm 55:22; Proverbs 16:9; 2 Corinthians 9:8; Ephesians 3:20; Philippians 4:19

Take Action: *So I am working on taking the word worry out of my vocabulary, my thoughts, and my heart, and replacing it with a better word: Jesus. Why don't you give it a try too?*

A Glimpse of God

Prayer Requests/Answers:
_____
_____
_____
_____

PATIENCE

Commitment: Gotta Run to Run

> Therefore, since we are surrounded by such a great cloud of witnesses, let us throw off everything that hinders and the sin that so easily entangles, and let us run with perseverance the race marked out for us.
> —Hebrews 12:1 NIV

I don't know a lot about running, but I do know it takes commitment. After my second son was born, I decided to take up running to help shed those excess pounds from pregnancy. After I put the kids down for a nap each day, I would try to run laps around my front yard. I started with three, not because the yard was enormous, but because I found out how out of shape I was.

But slowly, day after day, I ran and worked my way up to a mile, then several. For a while I even started lifting weights and trained to eventually run 5k races. I would get up early to get a run in before the kids were up or forgo one of my favorite TV shows at night to squeeze in some weight training. It took time and commitment. But I had to run to be able to run.

What you love, you will work hard to be good at. You will commit sleepless nights, tough training, and long days. You'll endure pain, injury, and hard situations to reach your goal, to obtain your prize whatever that might be. You don't learn or understand endurance without first learning what commitment looks like. As I learned when I was running, I had good runs and bad runs. Some days my body just didn't want to cooperate; some days it was my mind. Some exercises were painful while doing them (and for days later as well), but I could see my strength and endurance was increasing. As I have found out once I stopped training, I've had to start at the beginning to regain my strength and endurance.

I think the first thing I learned very quickly after becoming a Christian was that no matter how I tried, I couldn't and still can't run this life the way I should in my own power. The second thing I am learning is that only through His Spirit in me should I even try. When I do it on my own, I make mistakes and I don't always act like a Christ follower should. But when I allow His Spirit to work in me, the results are so much better. Philippians 1:6 (KJV), "Being confident of this very thing, that he which hath begun a good work in you will perform *it* until the day of Jesus Christ," has become one of my favorite promise Scriptures.

The third thing I am learning, however, is that I do have some part in all of this. I love my Lord and I have to have a higher level of commitment to Him. Some days I have a lot, and some days I don't. Just like those good runs and bad runs. I am learning I have to commit to read His Word and believe it even when others tell me different. I have to commit to let go of what I think I know, of doing it my way, and let God show me how it should be done. I have to commit to trusting Him during those sleepless nights or tough days that life sometimes brings me (even when the pain and tears last for days). "This is my command—be strong and courageous! Do not be afraid or discouraged. For the LORD your God is with you wherever you go" (Joshua 1:9 NLT). I have to commit to admit my sin, ask forgiveness, and believe Him when He says they're gone from His memory because He loves me that much. I have to commit to show His love to everyone and apologize when I don't. I have to commit to never stop trying to commit my life to Him.

More Scriptures: Psalm 37:5; Proverbs 16:3; 1 Corinthians 9:24–27; Hebrews 6:10–15

Take Action: *So commit to keep pressing on, sometimes hurting, sometimes failing, and other times going great. The prize waiting for you is so much better than anything here.*

A Glimpse of God

Prayer Requests/Answers:
_____
_____
_____
_____

Endurance: I Want To!

> What is more, I consider everything a loss compared to the surpassing greatness of knowing Christ Jesus my Lord, for whose sake I have lost all things. I consider them rubbish, that I may gain Christ.
> —Philippians 3:8 NIV

Can I say what Paul says in the Scripture above? *I want to!* Can I say that everything and everybody takes a backseat to Jesus? *I want to!* Can I say it is more important to me to please God than it is to please others? *I want to!* Can I say that all I have is God's to do with what He wants, even if that means I give it up? *I want to!* "For what is a man profited, if he shall gain the whole world, and lose his own soul? or what shall a man give in exchange for his soul?" (Matthew 16:26 KJV).

Can I say when something or someone in my life is no longer there, I can still give thanks and praise to God? *I want to!* Can I say even though I grieve for the loss, the grief does not overwhelm my thoughts so that it clouds my view of the prize? *I want to!*

> I'm not saying that I have this all together, that I have it made. But I am well on my way, reaching out for Christ, who has so wondrously reached out for me. Friends, don't get me wrong: By no means do I count myself an expert in all of this, but I've got my eye on the goal, where God is beckoning us onward—to Jesus. I'm off and running, and I'm not turning back.
> —Philippians 3:14 MSG

A Glimpse of God

Can I say even when it is hard and I get weary serving Him, I won't give up? *I want to!*

> By your *endurance* you will gain your lives.
> —Luke 21:19 NASB (emphasis mine)

> Let us not loose heart in doing good, for in due time we will reap if we do not grow weary.
> —Galatians 6:9 NASB

So I ask the question, How does the verse Philippians 3:8 (above) become true in my life?

> So he said to me, "This is the word of the LORD to Zerubbabel: 'Not by might nor by power, but by my Spirit,' says the LORD Almighty."
> —Zechariah 4:6 NIV

> But thanks be to God! He gives us the victory through our Lord Jesus Christ. Therefore, my dear brothers, stand firm. Let nothing move you. Always give yourselves fully to the work of the Lord, because you know that your labor in the Lord is not in vain.
> —1 Corinthians 15:57–58 NIV

The work is His, through His Spirit. I just have to be patient and let Him do the work. And He will. And I look around and see that anything short of knowing Jesus Christ is second-rate at best.

More Scriptures: 1 Corinthians 9:24–27; 15:57; James 1:12

Take Action: *I want to! Do you?*

Debra Niswander

Prayer Requests/Answers:

Contentment: To Have or Have Not

> Not that I speak from want, for I have learned to be content in whatever circumstances I am.
> —Philippians 4:11 NASB

Recently I was reading the book of Philippians in my morning devotions, which also is one of my favorite books. This particular morning I was in chapter 4. I jotted down my thoughts about the verses that stuck out the most—verse 8, then 9, then 11 and 12, and finally 13. As my last thought, I simply wrote, "That's how to be content." I've gone back to that chapter and that page in my journal since then to again gain insight.

The longer I read the Bible, the more I see the divine order of the writings (2 Timothy 3:16). Some days they are just words and don't seem to relate to my life. But, on days like this one, the words just seem to connect, to make sense, to come alive, and it is one of those "aha" moments. You could picture the cartoon where the light bulb goes on above the person's head. That looked kind of like me on that particular morning. I wish I could say I had something to do with it, but I know it is God turning that light on for me.

> Finally, brethren, whatsoever things are true, whatsoever things *are* honest, whatsoever things *are* just, whatsoever things *are* pure, whatsoever things *are* lovely, whatsoever things *are* of good report; if *there be* any virtue, and if *there be* any praise, think on these things.
> —Philippians 4:8 KJV

If only I could live that verse daily. If I think on what is true, honest, and just, most of my struggles would be gone—or at least smaller.

We are given the mind of Christ. Those things listed in Philippians 4:8 are everything that Christ embodies. When Christ lives in our hearts, we are infused with everything that He is (1 Corinthians 2:11–16). Verse 16 says, "But we have the mind of Christ." It just blows my mind (no pun intended) that I have His mind. With that comes the ability to understand and trust His Word. And then Paul tells us simply in Philippians 4:9 to follow verse 8 and God's peace will be with us. Think. Do. Peace.

That brings us to verses 11 and 12. Paul had been rich and poor, hungry and full, and he learned the secret of contentment: Philippians 4:13 says, "I can do all things through Christ who strengthens me" (NKJV). It is not what we have or don't have that makes us truly happy. It's not the paths we are on but how we travel them and who we travel them with that brings us peace. It is not what we go through that teaches us contentment but who goes through it with us: *Jesus Christ.*

> Keep your lives free from the love of money and be content with what you have, because God has said, "Never will I leave you; never will I forsake you."
> —Hebrews 13:5 NASB

More Scriptures: 2 Corinthians 9:8; Philippians 4:7; 1 Timothy 6:6

Take Action: *Contentment is not circumstances or possessions. It is a mind-set. Jesus is that mind-set. Let Him be that for you.*

Prayer Requests/Answers:

_____
_____
_____
_____

Perspective: Who or What Are You Waiting On?

> but those who hope in the LORD will renew their strength. They will soar on wings like eagles: they will run and not grow weary, they will walk and not be faint.
>
> —Isaiah 40:31 NIV

This would be one of my favorite verses of all time. The King James Version, as well as several others, use the word *wait*. I looked up the translations used in the Bible of the word *wait*. The one used the most often and with the most significance was "having eagerness or great expectation toward God and the truth He wants to reveal about Himself" (my paraphrase).

> But as for me, I will watch expectantly for the LORD; I will wait for the God of my salvation. My God will hear me.
>
> —Micah 7:7 NASB

When I pray, am I just waiting for the answer? What if the answer comes differently than what I expected? What if the answer takes months, years, or never comes in this lifetime? During all the waiting, was I concentrating on the wrong thing? Should I actually have been waiting for the *Lord Himself*? "I wait for the LORD, my soul waits, and in his word I put my hope" (Psalm 130:5 NIV).

As a child at Christmastime, it was more about the presents (come on, you know you were the same way) than it was about who gave them. As I have grown and gained perspective, I now feel it's about being with the people I love that makes the holidays. The presents are an extra blessing. It's like icing on a cake.

For a long time after becoming a Christian, my focus tended to look for the answers to my prayers. It wasn't that I didn't love the Lord, but I was a lot like a child at Christmas. Maybe I'm finally growing up in the Lord and gaining perspective (at least I'm trying to). Lately, I've been trying to concentrate on God while I'm waiting for the answers—and spending that "waiting" time on the *One* I love and the *One* I know loves me. I fight hard not to revert back to needing the answer rather than just being in God's presence. I am finding the true blessing *is* His presence and the answers are just extra blessings. *He* is the icing on the cake!

"And now, *Lord*, what do I wait for? My hope is in *You*" (Psalm 39:7 NKJV, emphasis mine). Hope is not placed in the answers, but in the *One* who gives them.

> Our soul waiteth for the LORD: he *is* our help and our shield.
> —Psalm 33:20 KJV

More Scriptures: Psalm 27:14; 130:6; Isaiah 25:9; 30:18; 33:2; Romans 8:24–25; Hebrews 6:13–19

Take Action: *Come into the presence of God and gain perspective of your true blessings.*

Prayer Requests/Answers:
___
___
___
___

KINDNESS

Honey

> See that none of you repays another with evil for evil, but always aim to show kindness *and* seek to do good to one another and to everybody.
> —1 Thessalonians 5:15 AB

It's funny sometimes the things or events God uses to reveal Himself to us or perhaps teach us a lesson He wants us to learn. At first glance you look at the event in one way, but maybe as you reflect more on the event, you see God revealing a deeper lesson. Whatever it might be, it is to perfect and change us into the mirror image of Christ so others will see Him through us. One of mine was a horse ...

One summer we took several from our church youth group on a weeklong mission trip to downstate Michigan. Our group teamed up with other groups on various projects in the area. My work crew was assigned to an equine center that does therapy for mentally, emotionally, and physically challenged individuals. I love horses (I had one at one time), so this was an unexpected blessing for me, until the end of the first day.

I was bringing one of the draft horses into the barn for grooming. Her name was Honey and she was extraordinary. While bringing her in and getting her in position, I hesitated and she stepped on my foot (all 1,200 pounds of her). You guessed it, instant pain. It seemed like an eternity to get her turned around and off my foot. I limped around and yet attempted to help finish grooming her, trying to put on a brave face that I was fine, because the embarrassment was as tough to handle as the pain.

By the time we got back to our home base for the night, my foot was swollen and I could only put slight pressure on my heel. A nice, huge bruise had formed. How was I going to work tomorrow? How could I even get my shoe back on? My fear was ... it was broken. I was really beginning to think I might have to go to a hospital. During our evening devotions, our youth group prayed for me. I went to bed with a bruised, swollen, painful foot. When I woke up the next day, the swelling was completely gone. I could walk on it with no pain. The bruise was the only sign of my injury. We rejoiced in the answered prayer. Now you might think that the lesson was pray and trust God to heal. Well, that was part of it.

Our crew headed back to the equine center. And guess what our first job was? To clean out Honey's paddock. I had to help the horse that hurt me. Told you God had a sense of humor. When we got to the paddock, she was lying down. At first we thought she was just resting, but soon we realized something was wrong. The manager came out to check on her, indicating she was colicky. Having had a horse that did that, I knew it could be very serious.

We got her up and because I had been in this situation, the manager asked if I would walk her until they could get a volunteer walker to come. The thing about walking a colicky horse is that you have to *make* them walk, because they don't want to. So here I was being asked to help this horse that just the day before hurt me. Although she had caused me pain, she needed me. How was I to respond? Of course, I helped. But since she really couldn't talk, I had time to think while walking. (I did also sing to her, however, which I believe she thoroughly enjoyed!) I thought how ironic it was to be helping the one that hurt me. Having to put aside the hurt and answering that hurt with an act of kindness.

I think you probably know where I'm heading with this analogy. How sometimes we are asked to put aside the hurt a friend, a parent, a loved one, a coworker, or even a stranger has caused us, to forgive and to answer with an act of kindness. To show love to someone who in some circumstances didn't deserve that love. You may be thinking that my little incident can't compare to some of the cruelties some have inflicted on others, on maybe even you. It's not always that simple. I was thinking the same thing, because I have found it hard on many occasions to respond with forgiveness, much less kindness. So I listened and allowed God to speak to me.

God's answer: *I really know it's hard, but it can be done. I did it once for all of you. The stripes on My back and the nail scars in My hands are a reflection of My act of kindness to the hurt and sin man caused by his rejection of Me. I have known your pain. Because of what I did, when you need the strength to forgive and answer in love, you can because you will do it through Me.* So I had to smile about how God could use a horse to again remind me of the length He went through to show His love for me. What a life-altering act of kindness that was!

> But when the kindness and love of God our Savior appeared, he saved us, not because of righteous things we had done, but because of his mercy. He saved us through the washing of rebirth and renewal by the Holy Spirit.
> —Titus 3:4–5 NIV

More Scriptures: Romans 12:17–21; 1 Peter 3:8–11

Take Action: *My lesson (maybe yours as well) is that I can answer to hurts with kindness when His Spirit in me produces that act of kindness. I just have to be open to His Spirit leading me.*

Prayer Requests/Answers:
_____
_____
_____
_____

Nothing Random about It

> You are the light of the world. A city set on a hill cannot be hidden; nor does *anyone* light a lamp and put it under a basket, but on the lampstand, and it gives light to all who are in the house. Let your light shine before men in such a way that they may see your good works, and glorify your Father who is in heaven.
> —Matthew 5:14–16 NASB

I like to hear the reports of the random acts of kindness. One such act was that during the Christmas season, people were paying other people's layaway bills. It was pretty cool. I wonder what they thought when they were told their debt was paid in full? However, I think we should call them intentional acts of kindness, not random. *Random* means without aim or purpose. But those acts, as well as others we've heard of or maybe we've done ourselves, all have had a purpose: to give someone some relief, to show them someone cares, or to give them hope. Yes, maybe sometimes a person does something for a stranger, but the *act* itself is intentional.

Some of you might know where I'm heading. The ultimate act of kindness was the one our heavenly Father did for us when He sent His Son as a sacrifice for our sins for the debt we could not pay. It was completely intentional and planned since before time (Ephesians 1:4–5; Romans 8:29). His purpose was most deliberate: to give us relief from our sin, to show us how much He cares, and to give us hope through this life and into the next. And He did not do it for His own recognition but for the glory of His Father.

I was almost done writing this when I came across a quote from a former mayor of Seattle, Washington, by the name of Norman Rice: "Dare to reach out your hand into the darkness, to pull another into

A Glimpse of God

the light." Jesus dared to reach into the darkness of sin and bring us into His light (John 8:12; 12:46; Titus 3:4–6). All He asked in Matthew 5:14–16 is for us to show what we have received from Him to help bring others out of their darkness and into His light as well. It is not about our recognition of the kindness we do, but the fact that others see God in that kindness—and not just at holidays, but every day.

> Dear children, let us not love with words or tongue but with actions and in truth.
> —1 John 3:18 NIV

More Scriptures: Mark 4:21; John 15:8; Ephesians 2:10

Take Action: *Through Him let all our acts of kindness be intentional. In all that we say and do, to all that we know and meet.*

Prayer Requests/Answers:
_____
_____
_____
_____

What If

> So, as those who have been chosen of God, holy and beloved, put on a heart of compassion, kindness, humility, gentleness, and patience.
> —Colossians 3:12 NASB

What if ... before we look at someone in disgust because they're different than us or we don't like them, we look at them the way God looks at them and at us because He loves them as much as He loves us? "Do nothing out of selfish ambition or vain conceit, but in humility consider others better than yourselves" (Philippians 2:3 NIV). What if we pray for them instead?

What if ... before we are critical of others, we are critical of ourselves first? "Why do you look at the speck that is in your brother's eye, but do not notice the log that is in your own eye? Or how can you say to your brother, 'Let me take the speck out of your eye,' and behold, the log is in your own eye?" (Matthew 7:3–4 NASB). What if we pray for them instead?

What if ... before we "judge" a person's actions, we find out what caused them to make those decisions in the first place, and then help them to make better decisions next time? "Let him know that he who turns a sinner from the error of his way will save a soul from death and cover a multitude of sins" (James 5:20 NKJV). And what if we pray for them too?

What if ... before we say something we don't like about a person, we say something nice about them instead? *And* say it to them. Why is it so easy to say something mean behind a person's back than it is to say something encouraging to their face? "Be kind to one another, tender-hearted, forgiving each other, just as God in Christ also has forgiven you" (Ephesians 4:32 NASB). And what if we pray for them too?

What if ... before we start an argument, we just don't? "A soft answer turns away wrath, but a harsh word stirs up anger" (Proverbs 15:1 NKJV). What if we pray instead?

What if ... we show God's love and kindness always to whoever we meet and whoever we know—even if they don't show it back? "Dear children, let us not love with words or tongue but with actions and in truth" (1 John 3:18 NIV). And what if we pray for them too? "A heart of compassion, kindness"—isn't that God's heart toward us?

I don't write these words lightly, because as I am writing them I have to repent from each and every one of them. This has come out of many discussions with my son on being who I say I want to be as a Christian. My hope is as I acknowledge them to myself and God, I can begin and end each day with a new effort to show kindness to all. Kindness is not kindness when you do it with contempt in your heart. It is kindness when you do it because when you look into that person's eyes, you see Christ and realize the price He paid for you and the kindness He showed you!

More Scriptures: Proverbs 17:17; Matthew 5:11; Romans 12:9–10

Take Action: *What if ... starting today we let kindness to **all** be the norm in our lives?*

Prayer Requests/Answers:
_____
_____
_____
_____

The Least of These

> but you will receive power when the Holy Spirit has come upon you; and you shall be witnesses both in Jerusalem, and in all Judea, and in Samaria, and even to the remotest part of the earth.
> —Acts 1:8 NASB

Most who know me, know that mission work is one of my passions. I believe mission work showcases everything that a Christian should be doing in respect to the Lord's work: evangelism, teaching, encouragement, service work, and so on.

I love to be involved in missions in my church. Right now I work with others in the Matthew 25 project. Throughout the year, we spend time helping people in the community with work projects. In describing the project to the youth group, I used the Acts 1:8 Scripture and substituted our hometown (Charlevoix, Michigan) for Jerusalem, "Michigan" for Judea, the "United States" for Samaria, and of course the whole world. I tried to emphasize the fact that Jesus didn't give us only one area to witness and serve in, He gave us everywhere, all at the same time. We do work in our own backyard, we do work farther away, but it's all going on at the same time. All are equal; all must be reached.

> Then the King will say to those on His right, 'Come, you who are blessed of my Father, inherit the kingdom prepared for you from the foundation of the world. For I was hungry, and you gave Me *something* to eat; I was thirsty, and you gave Me *something* to drink; I was a stranger, and you invited Me in; naked and you clothed Me; I was sick, and you visited Me; I was in prison, and you came to Me."
> —Matthew 25:34–36 NASB

I believe mission work is part of every aspect of our lives. *We* are missionaries each and every day in everything that we do. Each day we run into someone (and I don't believe those meetings are ever a coincidence) who fits this Scripture. Maybe the person is not physically hungry, but maybe he or she is spiritually hungry and we can give him or her words that feed their soul. "And Jesus said unto them, I am the bread of life" (John 6:35 KJV). It might be someone who needs a helping hand—maybe it is something so unremarkable like giving a ride to the store, or raking a yard, or simply taking time to visit. Maybe we meet someone who faces the walls of a prison, but it doesn't compare to the bars around their heart. Or just maybe we meet someone who, although he or she isn't surrounded by iron bars, that person is in prison nonetheless, and by introducing Jesus to either of these prisoners, He sets them free from their chains and gives them real life that no type of bars can take away. "So if the Son makes you free, you will be truly free" (John 8:36 NCV).

"Then the King will answer, 'I tell you the truth, anything you did for even the least of my people here, you also did for me'" (Matthew 25:40 NCV). Honestly, haven't we all at one time been the least of these?

More Scriptures: Proverbs 14:31; Matthew 25:37–46; James 1:27; 2:14–18

Take Action: *Show the love of Christ to each and every person you meet each and every day.*

Prayer Requests/Answers:
_____
_____
_____
_____

GOODNESS

Permanent and Inseparable

> But the other criminal stopped him and said, "You should fear God! You are getting the same punishment he is. We are punished justly, getting what we deserve for what we did. But this man has done nothing wrong." Then he said, "Jesus, remember me when you come into your kingdom." Jesus said to him, "I tell you the truth, today you will be with me in paradise."
>
> —Luke 23:40–43 NCV

My thoughts went to the thief on the cross for the quality of goodness. In experiencing and trying to study the Word as well as reading biblical scholars, it seems the fruit appear to be in groups or clusters—three to be exact. The first three express our relationship to God. As we experience true and pure love through our relationship with God, this gives us joy and peace internally and then we can express them outwardly. The next three seem to involve the you-to-me and the me-to-you relationships. As we allow the Spirit full access, kindness, patience, and goodness are shown to others. The last three seem to be our relationship within ourselves, while understanding that each of these qualities comes through the work of the Holy Spirit in us.

As is each fruit, goodness is an inherent quality of God. I looked up the word *inherent* and found the meaning to essentially say this: something that exists in someone that is permanent and inseparable. Basically, when you think of someone, you immediately think of that quality being them. When we say the phrase, "That man or woman is a good person," we mean that it is not what they do but who they are.

So I take you back to the thief. Matthew 27:44 and Mark 15:32 describe both thieves mocking Jesus with the others. But it seems as they both continue to suffer this fate on the cross, one thief really begins to look at Jesus and finally he sees God and man. He stops mocking Him and starts praying to Him. I believe that Jesus' response to the thief is a wonderful example of the inherent (permanent and inseparable) goodness of God. "I will see you in paradise." Forgiveness, love, patience, and kindness are displayed immediately without reservation despite how the thief had previously treated Him. Because of God's inherent goodness, it is who He is, and because of that, it is what He does. His only response is love and forgiveness, and it always is. We choose to accept or reject that goodness.

I have to admit that I am not good all the time and I do not return goodness every time I am offended. *I do not possess* that inherent quality. All of us can show goodness to each other, but it is neither permanent nor inseparable in us as we can see by the condition of the world. We certainly can do good things, but it is not engrained in our being as it is in God. However, when we accept Christ, He makes us a new creature (2 Corinthians 5:17), and because of that He gives us His inherent nature. As we surrender ourselves completely and allow the Holy Spirit to work in and through us, then the fruits can truly be seen as inherent in us.

More Scriptures: 2 Corinthians 5:21; Ephesians 2:8–10; 4:20–24; Colossians 3:1–25

Take Action: *Let us surrender ourselves and allow the permanent and inseparable goodness of God to be in us and shown to others.*

Prayer Requests/Answers:

Out of the Gutter

> He lifted me out of the slimy pit, out of the mud and mire; he set my feet on a rock and gave me a firm place to stand.
>
> —Psalm 40:2 NIV

A friend of mine gave me a great analogy the other day. We were talking about the need many of us have to help fix people. We end up in friendships or situations because we look at the other person and think we can help them. That's not necessarily a bad thing, but sometimes we get dragged down in the process. That's when my friend used the analogy that it's like seeing someone sitting in the gutter, and you lean over and extend your hand to help. But instead of pulling them out, you get pulled in because the one sitting in the gutter actually has all the leverage.

For a long time after our phone call had ended, I thought about that analogy and how it fits our relationship with God. I believe this world isn't as it was created to be. Read the story of creation, at the end of the third day it reads, "And God saw that it *was* good" (Genesis 1:12 KJV). And on the sixth day it ends with, "And God saw everything that he had made, and behold, it *was* very good" (Genesis 1:31 KJV). Adam had one rule to keep and he chose to disobey. We've been in the gutter ever since. In our own strength, we cannot keep ourselves or others from staying out of the gutter. And let's not think too poorly of Adam, for he is a reflection of all of us. "But we are all as an unclean *thing*, and all our righteousnesses are as filthy rags; and we all do fade as a leaf; and our iniquities, like the wind, have taken us away." (Isaiah 64:6 KJV). We might try to convince ourselves differently, but if we had been Adam, it would have been the same outcome. "I know that nothing good lives in me, that is, in my sinful nature. For I have the desire to do what is good, but I cannot carry it out" (Romans 7:18 NIV).

And so God, out of the goodness of His heart, actually chose to get in the gutter with us, understanding we could not get out on our own: "But God demonstrates his own love for us in this: While we were still sinners, Christ died for us" (Romans 5:8 NIV). He took on the stench of the gutter and He changed the gutter instead of it changing Him (Romans 8:38–39). And He's got the leverage now. So He extends His nail-scarred hand and pulls us up out of the gutter. He takes His goodness and gives it to us.

> You are kind and forgiving, O Lord, abounding in love to all who call to you.
> —Psalm 86:5 NIV

More Scriptures: Psalm 25:8–11; 136:1–3; Romans 5:6–7

Take Action: *When we accept God's grace, His goodness flows in and through us. Just reach up; His hand is always there. Just take it.*

Prayer Requests/Answers:
_____
_____
_____
_____

New Heart, New Eyes

> And I will give them one heart, and I will put a new spirit within you; and I will take the stony heart out of their flesh, and will give them an heart of flesh: That they may walk in my statutes, and keep mine ordinances, and do them: and they shall be my people, and I will be their God.
> —Ezekiel 11:19–20 KJV

Recently I was in a ladies' Bible group studying the Old Testament book of Ruth. Ruth lived during the period that was called the time of judges. The ongoing theme during that time period was, "but every man did *that which was* right in <u>his own eyes</u>" (Judges 17:6; 21:25 KJV, emphasis mine). And it usually ended in a disaster. Sounds like the world today doesn't it? "People may be right in their own eyes, but the LORD examines their heart" (Proverbs 21:2 NLT).

You cannot solve a "problem" with a solution from a world that has caused the "problem." To have new eyes, we need a new heart. Our hearts are diseased and that disease is called sin. The symptoms of that sin are what is played out day after day in this world: hate, abuse, murder (need I go on).

> Do you not understand that everything that goes into the mouth passes into the stomach, and is eliminated? But the things that proceed out of the mouth come from the heart and those defile the man. For out of the heart come evil thoughts, murders, adulteries, fornications, thefts, false witness, slanders.
> —Matthew 15:17–19 NASB

> For from within, out of men's hearts, come evil thoughts, sexual immorality, theft, murder, adultery, greed, malice, deceit, lewdness, envy, slander, arrogance, and folly. All these evils come from inside and make a man 'unclean.'"
>
> —Mark 7:21–12 NIV

The solution came on a starry night many years ago. It came in human form, but it was God as a human, one without a diseased heart. There is a saying, "out of the goodness of their heart." That's what Jesus did for us. He, out of the goodness of His heart, gave His life (John 3:16; Romans 5:8; 1 John 4:10). He laid His heart on a cross to destroy the disease of sin, thereby giving us a new heart with new eyes to see the world as *He* sees it. "I pray also that the eyes of your heart may be enlightened in order that you may know the hope to which he has called you, the riches of his glorious inheritance in the saints, and his incomparably great power for us who believe" (Ephesians 1:18 NIV).

God's truest desire for each of us is to know Him and His goodness and then to pass that goodness on to our fellow man. "Oh, that men would praise the Lord for his goodness, and for his wonderful works to the children of men. For he satisfieth the longing soul, and filleth the hungry soul with goodness" (Psalm 107:8–9 NKJV).

God's solution gives us the ability to have compassion for *all*, have love for *all*, and have a desire to help *all*. It is our choice to accept that solution, but until we all do, the "problem" will always be here.

More Scriptures: Psalm 119:18; Matthew 13:15; 2 Corinthians 3:3

Take Action: *Allow God to give you a new heart that looks like His. If you truly do, you'll never look at the world or yourself the same again.*

A Glimpse of God

Prayer Requests/Answers:
_____
_____
_____
_____

The Goodness of God

> For unto us a child is born, unto us a son is given: and the government shall be upon his shoulder: and his name shall be called Wonderful, Counsellor, The mighty God, The everlasting Father, The Prince of Peace.
>
> —Isaiah 9:6 KJV

> And she shall bring forth a son, and thou shalt call his name JESUS: for he shall save his people from their sins. … Behold, a virgin shall be with child, and shall bring forth a son, and they shall call his name Emmanuel, which being interpreted is, God with us.
>
> —Matthew 1:21, 23 KJV

I find it fitting that my last devotional for this book is one of goodness and I am writing it in the early hours of Christmas morning. Goodness. What is an example of the goodness of God? No, better yet, what is the essence of His goodness? For me, simply said, *grace*.

Grace is the underserved mercy from God, our Creator. It echoes across time. It came in flesh. "The Word became a human and lived among us. We saw his glory—the glory that belongs to the only Son of the Father—and he was full of grace and truth" (John 1:14 NCV). It calls out our names. It allows us to enter into everlasting life and it also allows us to stay there.

> *Because of his love*, God had already decided to make us his own children through Jesus Christ. That was what he wanted and what pleased him, and it brings praise to God because of his wonderful grace. *God gave that grace to us freely, in Christ, the One he loves.* In

A Glimpse of God

> Christ we are set free by the blood of his death, and so we have forgiveness of sins. *How rich is God's grace*, which he has given to us so fully and freely. God, with full wisdom and understanding, let us know his secret purpose. This was what God wanted, and he planned to do it through Christ.
> —Ephesians 1:5–8 NCV (emphasis mine)

Grab hold of the *goodness of God, His grace, His Son,* and *never* let go. At the end of the day, it is all we truly want and all we will ever need.

> And he said unto me, My grace is sufficient for thee: for my strength is made perfect in weakness. Most gladly therefore will I rather glory in my infirmities, that the power of Christ may rest upon me.
> —2 Corinthians 12:9 KJV

I am nothing without the grace of God, and I would rather be nothing than be without the grace of God.

More Scriptures: 1 Chronicles 16:8–10, 34; Psalm 100:1–5; 106:1

Take Action: *Any true fruit we bare in our lives, any holiness we show, is only because that grace is now in us.*

Prayer Requests/Answers:
_____
_____
_____
_____

FAITH

I Know That I Know That I Know

> I write these things to you who believe in the name of the Son of God so that you may know that you have eternal life.
>
> —1 John 5:13 NIV

I was around ten years old at the time. My mom and I picked up my Grandma Ethel and headed to the Hampton Roads Coliseum for an evangelistic crusade (whatever that was). By the time we got there the place was overflowing. I didn't think much about why we were going; I just knew my cousin would be there so we might have some fun. My cousin's mom had saved seats for my mom and grandma. My cousin, Mike, had a seat saved for me at the very top in the very last row, right next to this huge beam—undoubtedly to goof off out of view of our moms. I couldn't be any farther back in this place if I had tried.

My memories of going to church prior to this are nonexistent. I have a picture of my sisters and me dressed up for Easter, but I was so little I have no idea if we actually went to church. I do have a few recollections of attending vacation Bible school one summer, but nothing concrete. So this stuff about God was completely new to me.

For the most part my cousin and I paid about as much attention to the music and message as any red-blooded ten-year-olds would. I am sure the usher assigned to our area was about ready to hang us from that beam. But at some point during that service, the evangelist somehow got my attention. Something he said about who Jesus was (and is) and what He did for me stopped me in my tracks. I don't ever remember reading the Bible before that, but I was never so sure in my little life that the words he spoke were meant for me. It was like no one else was even there anymore. I wanted to know this Jesus he spoke of, to have Him in my life.

During the altar call as everyone had their eyes closed, the speaker asked for those who wanted to ask Jesus into their lives and be born again, to raise their hands. Mine shot up, tears streaming down my face. Then he asked that if we raised our hands to come down front and he would pray for us. My first thought was, "I'm not sure about that" (remember where I said I was sitting!), until he said that if you raised your hand and you didn't come, you would be making the biggest mistake of your life. And I knew he was right, even at ten. I knew that this would be the biggest decision I would ever make in my life. I just knew my life would be changed forever but only if I went down and asked Jesus into my heart. Please don't get me wrong. You can come to Christ anywhere you are, but I knew that I needed to make that move toward Him now—it couldn't wait. I didn't want it to wait. I had no idea what the changes would be, but it didn't matter; I just knew I wanted that. So I stepped out (my cousin did too!). I do remember the usher smiling and taking me to my mom and she walked down with me. At that point, I didn't care how far I had to walk; I just wanted to know Jesus. As I write this, I remember that feeling like it just happened.

I said the sinner's prayer with an altar worker: "Then I acknowledged my sin to you and did not cover up my iniquity. I said, 'I will confess my transgressions to the LORD'—and you forgave the guilt of my sin" (Psalm 32:5 NIV). They gave me papers and told me about Jesus. What an experience. No, there weren't any lightning bolts, no visions, but something inside me had changed, and I knew that. It was like a switch went on, and even though I knew very little about Jesus, I knew I knew Him. Someone once asked me, How do I know that I am born again? I can only say that *I know that I know that I know.* So go ahead, ask me. Do I still believe it was the biggest decision in my life? *Yes!* And the *best one* as well.

A Glimpse of God

But as many as received Him, to them He gave the right to become children of God, even to those who believe in His name.

—John 1:12 NASB

More Scriptures: Isaiah 43:25–26; Galatians 3:6

Take Action: *Step out and know that you know that you know!*

Prayer Requests/Answers:
_____
_____
_____
_____

Why I Write

> But Samuel replied: "Does the LORD delight in burnt offerings and sacrifices as much as in obeying the voice of the LORD? To obey is better than sacrifice, and to heed is better than the fat of rams."
> —1 Samuel 15:22 NIV

There I was making dinner, going over the conversation in my head that I had had earlier with a publishing company about several books I was writing. The company was the self-publishing kind. I was completely overwhelmed.

I laughed at myself—who was I to think I could get a book published? Yeah, maybe the children's books were a possibility; people are always looking for those. But this devotional was another matter. To think that these inspirations were from God, that He would give them to me. Who was I to write about God and who He is? Did I know enough to write about the Trinity and the fruit that His Spirit gives us? Would there be enough material for a book? I had no college or formal writing classes. How could I think that people would want to read my devotions? I must be nuts.

That's when God interrupted my pity party. He posed two questions. First, *if I give you these to write and only your family and friends see them, will you write them because I ask?* I started sobbing right in the middle of the goulash I was making and answered, "Yes, Lord." Second, *If I give you these to write and no one sees them, will you write them because I ask?* My answer: "Yes, Lord."

So I write because He asked!

A Glimpse of God

> But I gave them this command: Obey me, and I will be your God and you will be my people. Walk in all the ways I command you, that it may go well with you.
> —Jeremiah 7:23 NIV

More Scriptures: Hosea 6:6; Mark 12:28–34

Take Action: *Sometimes the biggest act of faith is a simple act of obedience.*

Prayer Requests/Answers:
_____
_____
_____
_____

A Little Boy, a Little Prayer, a Lot of Sun

> Now this is the confidence that we have in Him, that if we ask any thing according to His will, he hears us.
> —1 John 5:14 NKJV

If you are like me, over the years, certain stories of your children have become treasures. You love to share them with others. I have one (okay, more than one) such story about Jason, my younger son. When this incident happened, at first I tried to use it as a life lesson for Jason about thanking God when He answers our prayers. Over the years, it's also become a story showing Jason's unique character and a young child's way of looking at things.

Here is this mother's story. Jason was about three or four at the time. We were sitting at Daytona Beach. He was so excited about playing in the ocean, but the day was not really cooperating. It was cloudy, windy, and a little chilly. I was sitting on a blanket, while he was playing in the sand, not yet sure he wanted to venture into the waves. After a little while he came over to me and said, "Mom, I wish the sun would come out." My reply was, "Well, why don't you ask Jesus to make the sun come out?"

Right there on the beach, he bowed his head and prayed, "Jesus, help the sun to come out." I am not kidding you—instantly, back behind me and to my left the clouds parted over this tall hotel and the sun came through the clouds. Jason started pointing and shouting, "Mom, Mom, look! The sun is coming out!" Naturally, this is when I tried to teach that lesson I mentioned above, so I said, "Jason, that is great. Now, you have to thank Jesus." And as only Jason could respond, his reply was, "Why? I did all the work." I had to turn my head so he wouldn't see me burst out laughing. Then he promptly ran into the waves.

Of course, God answered the prayer and brought the sun out (you'll never convince me that was a coincidence), and He certainly deserves the praise for the answered prayer. But I admit, I have always thought about Jason's comment about doing the work. What work? I have come to believe there is a second life lesson here. It's the work of faith. I don't believe that faith is to be inactive, but it should be interactive with God Himself.

If we believe God to be all He is, then we should realize He really doesn't need our help. So why does He tell us to ask? It is because He loves to interact with us. God wants us to make that effort, to interact with Him, to step out and talk with Him. He wants to hear our desires, our hopes, and our frustrations. And you then say, "Well, if He's God, He already knows." You're right, but by interaction (prayer, praise, worship, etc.) we acknowledge to Him, to others, and especially to ourselves that we believe who He says He is in Hebrews 11:6: "And without faith it is impossible to please God, because anyone who comes to him must believe that *he exists* and that he rewards those who earnestly seek him" (NIV, emphasis mine). Faith cannot stand still. It must walk, and walking takes work. It takes interaction with the God we believe in.

Does that mean all answers come that quick or come the way we want them to? The answer is no. I've prayed enough to know. I read a great little book by Moody Press entitled *Son-Ripened Fruit*. In it there is a sentence that reads, "To experience God's peace, we must deliberately will to believe God's promises." I've got that sentence hanging on my wall at work, along with Romans 8:28: "And we know that all things work together for good to them that love God, to them who are the called according to *his* purpose" (KJV). I believe that is where 2 Corinthians 5:7 comes into play: "(For we walk by faith, not by sight)" (KJV).

More Scriptures: 1 Timothy 6:12; James 2:23–26

Take Action: *So put your faith to work and interact with God. He loves to interact with you.*

Prayer Requests/Answers:
_____
_____
_____

A Sister's Faith

The Lord *is* my shepherd; I shall not want.
—Psalm 23:1 KJV

When people see my sister, Crystal, most see a developmentally disabled person. Some look at her with pity, and I'm sure some even look down at her.

What do I see? I see a miracle. The doctors' prognosis for her as a child was that she would never walk or talk. Anyone who knows Crystal knows she has far surpassed that prognosis. But the amazing thing I really see in Crystal is her faith in Jesus Christ. She is unrelenting in her belief that Jesus loves her and died on the cross for her. She knows without a doubt she is going to heaven.

She doesn't complain that she's not like everyone else, can't live on her own, can't read or write, can't marry or have children. Those things don't seem to bother her. You might say it is because she just doesn't understand it, but I believe that she embodies the first verse of David's Psalm 23. She knows she is a child of God and she doesn't have to want for anything else. I've had her tell me, "Well, that's all right; that's the way God made me."

A nurse once described to me the difficulty one of her patients was having with her disability as "her deficiencies keep her from realizing she has deficiencies." I believe what we might see as the reasons Crystal wouldn't understand her disabilities are the reasons why she can believe so purely in Jesus. Her disabilities don't keep her from worshipping God; they *allow* her to worship God. I believe she might actually know something we don't and wish we did.

I have begun to count it a blessing to be next to her when she worships God during a church service. The look on her face radiates a look of pure joy. As Max Lucado says in his book, *The Applause of Heaven*, she has "reached the summit." She doesn't doubt God's love and that's enough for her. Oh, that it would be enough for each of us.

> Oh, taste and see that the LORD *is* good; blessed *is* the man *who* trusts in Him!
> —Psalm 34:8 NKJV

More Scriptures: Jeremiah 17:7–8; John 20:29; Romans 10:9

Take Action: *Take a lesson from Crystal. Let the Lord become your shepherd and want for nothing else.*

Prayer Requests/Answers:
_____
_____
_____
_____

GENTLENESS/ MEEKNESS (HUMILITY)

Meekness Is Not Weakness

> For he shall grow up before him as a tender plant, … He is despised and rejected of men. … and the LORD hath laid on him the iniquity of us all. … He was oppressed, and he was afflicted, yet he opened not his mouth.
>
> —Isaiah 53:2–3, 6–7 KJV

> Then Pilate asked Him again, saying, "Do You answer nothing? See how many things they testify against You!" But Jesus still answered nothing, so that Pilate marveled.
>
> —Mark 15:4–5 NKJV

Can you imagine the strength it took for Jesus to stand there and not defend Himself? He, God in the flesh, having to listen to the insults, the lies, the accusations, not to mention endure the physical assault, when with just one word everything and everyone could have been wiped off the face of the earth at that very moment. Although at the time He might have been viewed as weak by His accusers, nothing was further from the truth. His choice to endure all of it was prompted by love not weakness.

> Let this mind be in you which was also in Christ Jesus, who, being in the form of God, did not consider it robbery to be equal with God, but made Himself of no reputation, taking the form of a bondservant, *and* coming in the likeness of men. And being found in appearance as a man, He humbled Himself and became obedient to *the point of* death, even the death of the cross.
>
> —Philippians 2:5–8 NKJV

> In the beginning there was the Word. The Word was with God, and the Word was God. He was with God in the beginning. All things were made by him, and nothing was made without him. In him there was life, and that life was the light of all people.
> —John 1:1–4 NCV

His purpose was divine, in place before time existed. There was no weakness in His meekness, just obedience. "For as by one man's disobedience many were made sinners, so also by one Man's obedience many will be made righteous" (Romans 5:19 NKJV), or as it is written in *The Message* translation:

> Here it is in a nutshell: Just as one person did it wrong and got us in all this trouble with sin and death, another person did it right and got us out of it. But more than just getting us out of trouble, he got us into life! One man said no to God and put many people in the wrong; one man said yes to God and put many in the right.

Now that's strength—a divine strength coupled with a sensitivity of knowing our shortcomings before we even know them and demonstrating grace and mercy instead of retaliation. "You know the generous grace of our Lord Jesus Christ. Though he was rich, yet for your sakes he became poor, so that by his poverty he could make you rich" (2 Corinthians 8:9 NLT).

Every moment I think about what He did for me, the more I am amazed He did it. I am so amazed He is my God. My prayer is that I can allow His Spirit to infuse me so that I can display that kind of strength in tough situations.

A Glimpse of God

For God called you to do good, even if it means suffering, just as Christ suffered for you. He is your example, and you must follow in his steps.
—1 Peter 2:21 NLT

More Scripture: Matthew 11:28–31; Romans 8:17–18; 1 John 2:6–7

Take Action: *Dare we exclude this fruit?*

Prayer Requests/Answers:
_____
_____
_____
_____

Remember Where You Were

> As a prisoner for the Lord, then, I urge you to live a life worthy of the calling you have received. Be completely humble and gentle; be patient, bearing with one another in love.
> —Ephesians 4:1–2 NIV

So I am going to be a little critical of us as a Christian community—*and* I do include myself in this criticism. If nothing else, through my writings, God has exposed to me in a deeper way how I cannot, in myself, live a Christian life even in the simplest ways. I mess up so many times, so many days. I am learning I *must* continually and willingly surrender my will to God's Spirit within me. I am most thankful for the reminder that "Because of the LORD's great love we are not consumed, for his compassions fail not. They are new every morning; great is thy faithfulness" (Lamentations 3:22–23 NIV, emphasis mine).

Much of the world looks at us Christians as hypocrites, and sometimes rightly so. Could it be because we place judgment on them for their sin, but at the same time we are committing our own? I've done it. We as Christians have come to see how much our flesh wars with our spirit every day of our lives. But have we forgotten where we came from? Have we forgotten the sweet release of the weight of sin off our own hearts when we first met Jesus and how that forgiveness is daily? "My little children, these things I write unto you, that ye sin not. And if any man sin, we have an advocate with the Father, Jesus Christ the righteous" (1 John 2:1 KJV).

Have we become like the Israelites' religious leaders of biblical times, who instead of approaching the world and saying to them, "Look, we have met God, let us share His love and joy with you," instead gave the people a religion that was only punitive and void of love, all the while telling the people how terrible they were and that condemnation awaited them? It is certainly our calling as born-again Christians to tell others of Christ (Matthew 28:19–20), but I believe the Scriptures say it is the Spirit's job to convict someone of their sin, not our job to condemn. "For God sent not his Son into the world to condemn the world; but that the world through him might be saved" (John 3:17 KJV).

How do we present the gospel of Christ in a way that the world will desire it? I asked myself that question on my first trip to Africa. I posted on Facebook how at first I was overwhelmed with what to share with these people. What did I know of their lives or hardships? And I realized that all I could give them was Jesus. That is what this world needs. Whether it is the people in the village, my neighbor next door, my coworker, or anyone else I meet. *Always trying to humbly* remember where I was without Christ and allowing God's presence and love to be reflected in me. It is *God* who began and will continue to do His work in me (Philippians 1:6; Hebrews 12:2). I must bring nothing but a surrendered will and a heart that is open to His will. Only then will the world see not a religion, but a relationship and seek the same thing.

More Scripture: Proverbs 22:4; Lamentations 3:19–23; Romans 5:6–11; Ephesians 2:8–9; James 1:21–27

Take Action: *Let us show the world our relationship with Christ through love and humility.*

Prayer Requests/Answers:
_____
_____
_____
_____

Some Humble Pie

> Brethren, if a man be overtaken in a fault, ye which are spiritual, restore such an one in the spirit of meekness, considering thyself, lest thou also be tempted. Bear ye one another's burdens, and so fulfill the law of Christ.
> —Galatians 6:1–2 KJV

My self-examination continues into how we, in the Christian community, treat each other. The King James Version directs us "in the spirit of meekness" to restore other Christians who find themselves in trouble. Paul says to consider ourselves because we could be tempted as well. How often do we ask the Lord to reveal anything wrong in our lives before we speak into someone's life what they are doing wrong? Before we remove the speck in our brother's eye, are we checking to see if there's a plank in our own? Do we consider the battle we *all* fight daily? I cringe just thinking how often I've judged another, when I know I've done something wrong myself. I, for one, have to crucify myself daily, and unfortunately some days I just don't. Isn't it wonderful that He is a merciful God who offers forgiveness to *all* who seek it (1 John 2:1–2)?

You might say Jesus was very critical of the Pharisees and Sadducees during His life here. They were the religious leaders of that time. It seems to me most of His criticism was directed at how they treated others in the name of religion while abusing that religion themselves by their own behavior. As Christians, each of us is called a royal priest. We are the religious leaders of our time (1 Peter 2:5, 9). If Jesus were to live on earth now, would He be critical of us? Are we showing others an empty religion or a true relationship through our Lord and Savior?

A Glimpse of God

Paul used the word *restore*. Is that our goal as Christians when someone fails? Are we looking at that person with the same intensity of love that the Father looks at us when we fail? Do we just want their relationship with Him to be right again? Before we pick up the stone, are we looking at the writing in the sand (John 8:1–11)? If so, then maybe we would humbly and with love take that person's hand, and we would both bow at the altar of our God in a prayer of repentance and praise.

> My brothers, if one of you should wander from the truth and someone should bring him back, remember this: Whoever turns a sinner from his error will save him from death and cover over a multitude of sins.
> —James 5:19–20 NIV

More Scriptures: Romans 7:14–25; 8:1–2; 15:1–4; Ephesians 2:8–9

Take Action: *Humble pie may be difficult going down at first, but if it brings me closer to my Lord, I'll even try to handle a double portion. Want me to cut you a piece?*

Prayer Requests/Answers:
_____
_____
_____
_____

In Awe

> Then I said, "It's all over! I am doomed, for I am a sinful man. I have filthy lips, and I live among a people with filthy lips. Yet I have seen the King, the Lord of Heaven's Armies."
> —Isaiah 6:5 NLT

> God saved you by his grace when you believed. And you can't take credit for this; it is a gift from God. Salvation is not a reward for the good things we have done, so none of us can boast about it.
> —Ephesians 2:8–9 NLT

I don't know why, but reading these two Scriptures together brings me face-to-face with myself. It brings my soul to the brink of who I really was without Christ. I find myself standing at the precipice, acknowledging to myself this is who I am (I am doomed for I am a sinful person). And yet even in that exact same moment, I know that because Jesus put Himself between me and that precipice, my Creator, my Father smiles and welcomes me home (I am no longer doomed, I have been redeemed by the blood of my Savior). It takes my breath away thinking about how the holy God of heaven looks down on me and smiles for no other reason than because He chooses to. "*Such* knowledge is too wonderful for me; It is *too* high, I cannot attain to it" (Psalm 139:6 NASB).

It brings me back to a great truth. It is not *we* who have the right to measure sin, it is *God*, and because of that, no one measures up! We also do not have the right to measure self-worth; God does, and because of that, He treasures each of us individually!

A Glimpse of God

> O LORD, you have searched me and you know me. ... Where can I go from your Spirit? Where can I go from your presence? ... For you created my inmost being; you wove me in my mother's womb. I praise you because I am fearfully and wonderfully made; your works are wonderful, I know that full well. ... Search me, O God, and know my heart; test me and know my anxious thoughts. See if there is any offensive way in me, and lead me in the way everlasting.
> —Psalm 139:1, 7, 13–14, 23–24 NIV

Humbled I am. Father, forgive me when I don't remain that way.

> Don't you realize that your body is the temple of the Holy Spirit, who lives in you and was given to you by God? You do not belong to yourself, for God bought you with a high price. So you must honor God with your body.
> —1 Corinthians 6:19–20 NLT

More Scriptures: Psalm 89:6; Isaiah 66:2; Luke 18:9–14; Titus 3:1–7; James 4:6–10

Take Action: *Seek the true presence of God, Jehovah. Once you do, I guarantee you'll never look at yourself the same way again.*

Prayer Requests/Answers:
_____
_____
_____
_____

SELF-CONTROL

God-Control

> Trust in the Lord with all your heart and lean not on your own understanding; in all your ways acknowledge him, and he will make your paths straight. Do not be wise in your own eyes; fear the Lord and shun evil.
>
> —Proverbs 3:5–7 NIV

When God first inspired me to write this book, I always thought I would write it section by section: God the Father, God the Son, and so on. I am sure it was probably my organizational tendencies coming out. I also thought that once I understood the Trinity (why I ever thought my human brain could really grasp the infinite Godhead) I would then move on to the fruit of the Spirit. I believe my writings reflect that I have been learning the truth of what St. Thomas Aquinas said so many years ago: "There are two absolute mysteries in Christianity: the mystery of the incarnation and the mystery of the trinity." The understanding has little to do with the brain but much more to do with our spirit. Sometimes you can't explain it; you just have to believe it.

Most of what I write is what I am experiencing at the time, and I try to express how God relates it to *Him* and about me. I have looked forward to how He reveals Himself to me in my writings—many times repenting, but always praising Him. Sometimes I'll be working on one area of thought and end up writing something entirely different (kind of like now). The one area I seem to stay away from, the one I always fear, has been self-control. What could I write about self-control? It would be more like unself-control (like that is even a word). I've been known to "open mouth, insert foot" (my dad used to always call me the mouth from the south), or act before I think. Now, if I had written a book about all the times I have lacked self-control in my Christian walk, I could have had more than enough material to probably fill volumes.

So, I've tended to shy away from that fruit. I've thought that if I could work on myself through the other fruits, then maybe one day I would be better able to write on self-control. That is how this one came about. In the back of my mind, the idea of self-control kept popping up while I was working on another devotional. I kept trying to dismiss those thoughts, because I felt inadequate to write about this fruit knowing my lack of self-control at times. That's when God revealed to me that I was concentrating too much on the word *self* in self-control.

I gain self-control only by being God-controlled. I let Him control my thoughts, my actions, and my mouth. So I said to Him, "I know, Lord, but how do I ever get there? You know me better than anyone, and it seems like sometimes I don't have any. I go two steps forward some days, and other days, six million sets back." (Well, it feels like six million steps back.) He said, *One day at a time, one step at a time, one act at a time, one conversation at a time, one thought at a time. Think of Me first; think of yourself second. Let each thought be My thought, let each conversation be My conversation, let each act be My act, let each step be My step, let each day be My day.*

> Search me, O God, and know my heart: try me, and know my thoughts: And see if *there be any* wicked way in me, and lead me in the way everlasting.
> —Psalm 139:23–24 KJV

More Scriptures: 2 Corinthians 10:1–5; Philippians 4:8; Titus 2:11–12

Take Action: *"Okay, Lord, each day I'll try to let this day be <u>Your</u> day!"*

A Glimpse of God

Prayer Requests/Answers:
_____
_____
_____
_____

Stumbling

> The LORD delights in the way of the man whose steps he has made firm; though he stumble, he will not fall, for the LORD upholds him with his hand.
> —Psalm 37:23–24 NIV

I debated which version of Scripture to use here. King James puts verse 24 this way; "Though he fall, he shall not be utterly cast down: for the LORD upholdeth him with his hand." Whatever rears its ugly head in a Christian's life—stumbles, onetime incidents, and full-blown falls; or stumbling blocks like continual addictions, ongoing anger, depression issues, and unhealthy relationships—no one wishes to experience any of them. It can be very humbling. They hinder our relationship with God and affect our witness to others. Despite what we sometimes think, none of us are immune. And if we believe we are immune, it could be our first step to stumble or fall. What you deal with might not be what I deal with. "For whoever keeps the whole law and yet stumbles in one *point*, he has become guilty of all" (James 2:10 NASB).

> I know that nothing good lives in me, that is, in my sinful nature. For I have the desire to do what is good, but I cannot carry it out. For what I do is not the good I want to do; no, the evil I do not want to do—this I keep on doing.
> —Romans 7:18–19 NIV

We should try to deal with it—or should I say, let Christ deal with it—before the issues become a stumbling block, but sometimes we just don't. "I do not understand what I do. For what I want to do I do not do, but what I hate I do" (Romans 7:15 NIV). Our stumbling blocks can be removed, but only through the cross of Christ. The cross pulverizes our stumbling blocks into a million pieces, but we must willingly lay them down and leave them there. For whatever reason, we go back time after time and pick up a piece here and a piece there, and before we know it, that stumbling block is back together.

If I am honest, I'm like a moth that is attracted to the fire. The moth moves closer and closer to the fire, always thinking it can retreat if it gets too hot. But it gets close one too many times and that's when the flame reaches out to consume and destroy it. That fire is like a stumbling block.

> So, I say, live by the Spirit, and you will not gratify the desires of the sinful nature. For the sinful nature desires what is contrary to the Spirit, and the Spirit what is contrary to the sinful nature. They are in conflict with each other, so that you are not to do whatever you want.
> —Galatians 5:16–17 NIV

In facing a particular stumbling block of my own, God has really been dealing with me about moving closer to the fire of the Holy Spirit instead of the other flame. As I go toward the Spirit, I am less likely to want to go the other way. The difference is that with the fire from the Holy Spirit, He engulfs me and refines me, unlike the other fire, which consumes me and destroys me (1 Peter 1:6–7). His fire burns off the dregs and impurities of my sinful nature, and what is left is pure, for what is left is His Spirit in me.

I have to confess, it has been difficult, and I know it is because I try to do it on my own or in my own way instead of surrendering my will to His Spirit. I don't always like surrendering my will, but a pastor friend of mine said something to me that got me really thinking about the decision to walk away from anything, including a stumbling block, that hinders my relationship with Christ. He said, "Remember that you love Christ more than self," and he gave me the Scripture Philippians 3:13–14 (NIV).

> Brothers, I do not consider myself yet to have taken hold of it. But one thing I do: Forgetting what is behind and straining toward what is ahead, I press on toward the goal to win the prize for which God has called me heavenward in Christ Jesus.

And what peace overcomes you when you finally willingly release it to Christ. A weight has been lifted. We must not forget we truly are in the fight of our lives. Nothing in this world is worth losing our souls (Matthew 16:26).

More Scriptures: Psalm 139:23–24; Romans 8:26–28; Ephesians 6:10–18; Jude 24–25

Take Action: *Today, make a stand with me. We will strive to move closer to His Spirit. Our lives, as well as those of the others we witness to, depend on it.*

Prayer Requests/Answers:

_____
_____
_____
_____

C.A.R.P.

I love God's law with all my heart. But there is another power within me that is at war with my mind. This power makes me a slave to the sin that is still within me. Oh, what a miserable person I am! Who will free me from this life that is dominated by sin and death? Thank God! The answer is in Jesus Christ our Lord. So you see how it is: In my mind I really want to obey God's law, but because of my sinful nature I am a slave to sin.

So now there is no condemnation for those who belong to Christ Jesus. And because you belong to him, the power of the life-giving Spirit has freed you from the power of sin that leads to death.
—Romans 7:22–8:2 NLT

Oftentimes my life seems somewhat like a roller-coaster ride; holding on through the downslopes of defeat and disappointment by admitting my weaknesses and sin, and to the thrill of coming to the top in victory and forgiveness and hopefully growth in God. My devotionals have certainly reflected that.

It's hard to admit to a behavior the Holy Spirit has been trying to weed out, especially knowing I've been nothing but resistant in letting Him do that weeding. It's amazing how deep those roots can become. It's hard to face one's shortcomings sometimes. Those are the days that the idea of moving to a monastery is quite enticing—to escape the pressures of the world, and maybe, just maybe I can be a better Christian! Yet, I really know that is not the solution, because I would be taking myself with me, and I am most of my own problem. "But people are tempted when their own evil desire leads them away and traps them. This desire leads to sin, and then the sin grows and brings death" (James 1:14–15 NCV).

I feel exactly like the way Paul felt in the first part of the Scriptures above. It is miserable, or can be, to know that as hard as I try, I still get caught up in sin. And I used to think if Paul couldn't do it, how could I. I can see his struggles throughout his words, but I believe I finally see what he caught on to. I call it C.A.R.P.

"C"oncede—"I struggle in my Christian walk with my old nature" (paraphrase of verses 22–23). I love my Lord with all my heart. I want to do His will, but I've got this old part of me that fights me constantly and sometimes I let it lock me up again.

"A"dmit—"I'm a mess and can't do it myself" (paraphrase of verse 24a). I'm a mess this way. I'm weak. I *can't* do it.

"R"elinquish—"Surrender my pride and look for help" (paraphrase of verse 24b). I need help. *Who* can help me get out of this?

"P"eace—"Comfort and relief knowing I'm not alone and someone is fighting for me and delivering me" (paraphrase of verses 7:25–8:2). *I thank God* that *Jesus* does this for me, and although I struggle sometimes, I know He never stops loving me and He is working in me and I can stand strong when *I* walk *in Him* and not in myself.

> Give me back the joy of your salvation. Keep me strong by giving me a willing spirit.
> —Psalm 51:12 NCV

More Scriptures: Psalm 51; Romans 6:6–8; 8:36–39; 1 Corinthians 15:56–58; Galatians 2:20; 3:13; 5:1, 24–25; Colossians 2:6–15

A Glimpse of God

Take Action: *Find the catch of a lifetime through the Holy Spirit inside you!*

Prayer Requests/Answers:
_____
_____
_____
_____

To Die, Yet Live

> I have been crucified with Christ; it is no longer I who live, but Christ lives in me; and the *life* which I now live in the flesh I live by faith in the Son of God, who loved me and gave Himself for me.
> —Galatians 2:20 KJV

At times I have struggled with the path of my life. I guess sometimes I think some things are missing and I become disappointed. It happens when I compare the look of my life to the look of others' lives. Maybe I'm the only one, but I don't really think so.

I have found the problem with comparing my life to another's makes me forget or miss the blessings I already have or that I could have. It also leaves me open to depression, fear, anxiousness, anger, and the inability to see my own path. It makes me miss enjoying living in the moment and seeing how God can lead me in those moments. Have you ever felt that? My life isn't supposed to look like yours, and your life isn't supposed to look like mine. I know, you are probably saying, "Thank God for that."

Seriously though, God has made each of us unique with a life to be directed by Him (Psalm 37:23). When we are so busy looking at the wrong life, we get lost on the trail. We attempt to make our lives into something they were never meant to be, and because of that, peace eludes us. This is just a thought, but it doesn't work and it can cause damage to us and others that often takes a long time to repair. I have unfortunately done it. Maybe we should review our lives continually in the light of what God wants for us and not through the view of another person's life or what we think life should be like.

A Glimpse of God

God's view:

For I know the plans I have for you, declares the LORD, plans to prosper you and not to harm you, plans to give you a hope and a future.

—Jeremiah 29:11 NIV

We must daily trust our path to Him and He will direct it (Proverbs 3:5–6). Is it easy? No (as you can tell by my many confessions), but He never said it would be. Somehow we have come to believe that as a Christian, our paths aren't supposed to be difficult at times. He never said that either. What He did say was that to gain our true life we must lose our old life: "Those who try to hold on to their lives will give up true life. Those who give up their lives for me will hold on to true life" (Matthew 10:39 NCV). We were brought back to a right relationship with God at an enormous price—the life of Jesus Christ. He asks the same from us: our lives, and to let Him live through us. It is our choice, but as Paul says, we "die" to ourselves, and in doing so, we finally *truly live*. "For to me, to live is Christ and to die is gain" (Philippians 1:21 NIV).

More Scriptures: Luke 17:33; John 11:25–26; 12:24–26

Take Action: *Live your God-chosen path knowing that God is with you through whatever and wherever that path leads.*

Prayer Requests/Answers:
_____
_____
_____
_____

A Final Thought

Live Like You Believe It

Be still, and know that I am God.
—Psalm 46:10 KJV

"Be still" is translated to mean "stop striving."

I saw this bumper sticker once that said, "Live like You Believe It." They are five powerful words that over the years have really spoken to me. In fact, at times they have haunted me.

I can't "live like I believe it" if I continue to strive against God and tell Him *who I think* He should be and what He should do. In these devotions, you see the times I have strived, and also the times I have finally stopped. And when I did finally stop, I received the most extraordinary glimpses of who God is. I get up each day anticipating what He will reveal next. And I can't wait for the day when they won't be just glimpses but I'll stand in His presence and see Him face to face!

In the devotional titled "The Goodness of God," I made the statement, "I am nothing without the grace of God, and I would rather be nothing than be without the grace of God." I see it in my life through my everyday experiences, during my trials—the forgiveness of my sins and failures. My appreciation and love for God grows every day.

If in my journey so far there is a passage that has come to fit me, I would say this one is it:

> I'm not saying that I have this all together, that I have it made. But I am well on my way, *reaching out for Christ, who has so wondrously reached out for me.* Friends, don't get wrong: By *no means* do I count myself an

> expert in all of this, *but I've got my eye on the goal, where God is beckoning us onward—to Jesus. I'm off and running, and I'm not turning back.*
> —Philippians 3:14 MSG (emphasis mine!)

The group Big Daddy Weave sings a song entitled, "Redeemed." A part of the song goes like this:

> Because I don't have to be the old man inside of me
> 'Cause his day is long dead and gone
> Because I've got a new name, a new life, I'm not the same
> And a hope that will carry me home
>
> I am redeemed, You set me free
> So I'll shake off these heavy chains
> Wipe away every stain, 'cause I'm not who I used to be
> —Benji Cowart & Michael David Weaver

I make mistakes. I fail often, but I know I can count on God's love and grace. And because of that never-ending love and grace, I will continue to try to live like I believe it. That is the least I should do for my Savior. And I also know I can only do that through Jesus Christ and through Him alone. I continue to be a work in progress. He's not done with me yet. *I thank Jesus that He's not.*

The most exciting words I want to hear from my Father, my Savior, my Friend, my Lord are ... *Well done, thou good and faithful servant.*

God bless you, my friends,
Deb